Praise For
Champion for Charlie

"I'm praising God for *Champion for Charlie*. When we, as special-needs parents, feel tempted to give in and give up, Jen Forsthoff gives us page after page of Christ-centered encouragement and reminds us that 'we must get ourselves up, dust ourselves off, and move forward.' She also reminds us this cannot be done in our own strength, but only through an all-out encounter with Jesus. Thank you, Jen, for pointing us to Scripture and, in so doing, pointing us to our true Champion. Your words resonate with me deeply, both as an advocate for families impacted by disability and even more so as the one who has been chosen to be Sarah's mom."
—**Shauna Amick**, MEd, Director of Direct Response and Radio Channel Marketing, Joni and Friends International Disability Center

"It is a rare and wonderful thing to be deeply moved, convicted, and inspired by the same book. Jen Forsthoff's newest book, *Champion for Charlie*, is just such a book, and I recommend it heartily."
—**Dr. Mark Rutland**, Founder and Director of the National Institute of Christian Leadership, *New York Times* bestselling author

"As I read the first words and turned the pages of *Champion for Charlie*, my heart cried a resounding *Yes*! As a mother to a daughter with Down syndrome, I wanted to see a copy of Jen Forsthoff's book land in the home of every parent. No matter the personality, temperament, or diagnosis that has defined the children God has gifted you with, this book will bring you an eternal perspective of parenting that will give you the fortitude, hope, and empathy you need as you journey out your day-to-day. You will also find an elevated perspective that will expand your heart and potentially make our world a better place."
—**Jen Jones**, coach, author, speaker, and advocate for Addie, Founder of The Significant Conference, CEO at Jen Jones Direct

"Ever been captured by a book by the conclusion of the first few pages? Such will be your experience as you begin *Champion for Charlie* by Jen Forsthoff. My first meeting with Jen was walking into church and overhearing her loving encouragement to Charlie as she carefully made her way up the church steps. Jen's tender patience oozed from even the few words to her daughter that I overheard that morning. I thought to myself, *Behind that patience are countless price tags that this family bravely pays each day to care so lovingly for Charlie.* So my encouragement to you as you begin this exceptional book? I truthfully cannot think of a calling more honorable or more sacred than to be one of the human angels assigned to helping to raise a special-needs child. Happy reading and welcome to one of Heaven's most elite assignments: Being a champion for your Charlie."

—**Dr. Jeanne Mayo**, public communicator and author, Founder and CEO: Youth Leader's Coach, Founder of The Cadre and Legacy Leadership Coaching

"As a mother of three children and aunt to Charlie, this book hits multiple heartstrings at once. It reminds me of the amazing gift I have as a mother to have been chosen to parent each of my children. It calls me to renew my passion to not just get lost in the daily grind of parenting but fight to champion the purpose of my child's heart. In this honest, transparent, and passionate book, you will be stirred on all levels of parenting. Parenting is not for the faint of heart, but it is an invitation to truly champion the child(ren) our lives have been gifted. This book will blow fresh wind in your parenting sails as you forge forward with renewed hope."

—**Hannah Ouellette**, Founder of Flourish Women's Ministry, co-Pastor of Thrive Church in Parker, Colorado

"I've had the privilege to know Pastor Luke and Jen Forsthoff for nearly twenty years. Their purity of heart, sincere commitment to God's calling, and authentic leadership already demanded the utmost respect. Now, having watched their journey with their amazing Charlie, my appreciation for who they are has only expanded. In *Champion for Charlie*, you will be challenged, inspired, and equipped through the moving story of two parents whose trust in God not only carried them but also elevated them to a place of supernatural joy and peace. Their testimony is full of hope and speaks to us all."

—**Dominic Russo**, Founder of Missions.Me and 1Nation1Day

"Jen's heart of compassion for people is one of a kind. I believe her book will be a powerful tool in your hands. As you read each page, you will not only grow in purpose but also strength to be your child's champion."

—**Paul Daugherty**, Victory Lead Pastor, Tulsa, Oklahoma

"Jen Forsthoff presents a compelling and informative challenge to parents of special-needs children. *Champion for Charlie* not only walks you through her personal journey but Jen also provides spiritual and practical advice. This book inspires you to recognize your calling to advocate for your child, it helps you recognize issues that sidetrack you from advocating without peace, and it informs you how to advocate in almost every relational interaction you will encounter raising your child."

—**Bobby Bogard**, author of *Essentials: Bridging the Leadership Gap* and *Daily Essentials: Principles for Life Management*

Jen Forsthoff

Champion for Charlie

Rise Up and Advocate for Your Child

Champion for Charlie
© 2021 by Jen Forsthoff

All rights reserved. No part of this publication may be reproduced in any form or by any electronic or mechanical means, including information storage and retrieval systems, without permission in writing by the publisher, except by a reviewer who may quote brief passages in a review. For information regarding permission, contact jen@jenforsthoff.com.

> This book is available at special discounts when purchased in quantity for use as premiums, promotions, fundraisers, or for educational use. For inquiries and details contact jen@jenforsthoff.com.

Editing and Cover / Interior Design by My Writers' Connection
Cover Photography by Kendra Renee Photography
Published by Courageous Heart Press, College Station, Texas

Library of Congress Control Number: 2021948168
Paperback ISBN: 978-1-950714-17-9
Ebook ISBN: 978-1-950714-18-6

Scripture quotations marked (ESV) are from The ESV® Bible (The Holy Bible, English Standard Version®), copyright © 2001 by Crossway, a publishing ministry of Good News Publishers. Used by permission. All rights reserved.

Scripture quotations marked (NIV) are taken from the Holy Bible, New International Version®, NIV®. Copyright ©1973, 1978, 1984, 2011 by Biblica, Inc.™ Used by permission of Zondervan. All rights reserved worldwide. zondervan.com. The "NIV" and "New International Version" are trademarks registered in the United States Patent and Trademark Office by Biblica, Inc.™

Scripture marked (NKJV) taken from the New King James Version®. Copyright ©1982 by Thomas Nelson. Used by permission. All rights reserved.

Scripture quotations taken from the Amplified® Bible (AMP), Copyright ©2015 by The Lockman Foundation. Used by permission.

Living Bible (TLB) The Living Bible copyright © 1971 by Tyndale House Foundation. Used by permission of Tyndale House Publishers Inc., Carol Stream, Illinois 60188. All rights reserved.

Also by Jen Forsthoff

Chosen for Charlie

"With Jen's thoughtful, provocative, and insightful reflections on the specific calling of the special needs of each child, you will be encouraged to find fresh hope in your personal journey."
—**Sue Detweiler**, author of *9 Traits of a Life-Giving Mom*

"Jen Forsthoff has given us a most compelling, compassionate, and transparent insight into her incredible journey of faith. This book is a God-given gift that speaks to the heart!"
—**Kemp Holden**, chairman, Worldwide Evangelism

"*Chosen for Charlie* is a tremendous resource for every parent, grandparent, or anyone chosen to love and care for a special-needs child."
—**Becky Thompson**, author of *Hope Unfolding*

In Loving Memory of

My brother, Daniel, an advocate and champion
for his students at Atrisco Elementary,
and his niece, my daughter, Charlie.

Contents

Foreword		xiii
Introduction		xvii
Chapter 1	An Invitation to Rise Up	1
Chapter 2	Rise Up. Now What?	15
Chapter 3	Rise Up for What?	29
Chapter 4	Chosen to Champion	49
Chapter 5	Pray to Win	61
Chapter 6	The Grit of Gratitude	75
Chapter 7	Strength to Strength	87
Chapter 8	Advocate Allies Part 1—Parents and Ministry Leaders	99
Chapter 9	Advocate Allies Part 2—Teachers and Doctors	111
Chapter 10	The Ultimate Champion	125
Advocate Resource Page		135
Acknowledgments		139
About the Author		141

Foreword

I write this foreword from many perspectives, all of which matter when it comes to empathy and advocacy—two important aspects of living faithfully as a parent, friend, and Christian.

I am a past public high school teacher and current assistant professor of teacher education at John Brown University. I have spent countless hours in dozens of schools and have been entrenched in educational research for many years. I am active in a church community that seeks to serve members who have needs that are often overlooked by mainstream evangelical churches. From this perspective, I want to encourage you to read these pages and the practical and insightful steps they contain to becoming a champion for children with special needs in their school, work, places of worship, and extracurricular activities.

I am also a mother seeking to intentionally parent my children. My husband and I are always looking for ways to help our children empathize with others, find friends who are the same as them and who are different from them, and create space in our family and home for all of God's children. From this perspective, I invite you to read this as a message from a mother who longs to help you cultivate empathy and provide support for others as you articulate your own experience. Motherhood is riddled with internal and external pressures that many of us carry deep within our hearts. Let these pages be a window to see the experiences of another family, or a mirror to see your own experiences from a different viewpoint.

Finally, I am Jen Forsthoff's sister, and from this perspective, I can attest that the journey she recounts in this book has been walked with integrity, honesty, and humility. Jen and Luke have invested countless hours and led many rounds of explanations, corrections, and redirections for our entire family as they've mentored us in being champions for Charlie, for her siblings, and for them as her parents. Our family is in an ongoing state of learning, adjusting, listening, and having hard conversations, but we are able to persevere through it because of the example that Jen and Luke set for their children, church, and community.

Throughout our journey of growing in empathy and advocacy for people with special needs, our family has experienced moments of great challenge and intense clarity. One of those experiences happened rather unexpectedly and has served as a framework for me for the past several years. My hope is that it will also provide you with a framework, a sketch of sorts, and a way to see all that is involved in this work and the great opportunity that awaits you.

My husband and I have been part of a parachurch ministry for several years, and one of our responsibilities is directing college and university students who staff camps for young people of all ages and backgrounds. These camps serve high school students, middle school students, teen mothers, and kids with special needs from across the country. The ministry's motto is that camp is the best week of a camper's life, and there are no exceptions.

One summer, we had a large group of very special campers who required various accommodations, and by adjusting cabins, changing the schedule, and reworking meals, the entire camp pitched in and made space for everyone in that group. One day, I was standing near the pond at the back edge of the property with my two children (who were four and eight at the time). We heard a ruckus at the ropes course on the other side of the pond and ran to see what was happening.

The camp staff was all-hands-on-deck that afternoon to provide support for our campers with varying abilities as they navigated the ropes course. Their goal was to figure out how to get each camper to whatever part of the ropes course they wanted to attempt. One camper, whose arms and legs were not under his control, wanted to do the entire ropes course. Several highly trained camp staff members using advanced equipment slowly and carefully carried the camper through the entire course several stories above the ground, making adjustments and shifts to equipment so the camper could maneuver through every obstacle and reach every new height.

As my children and I watched and cheered, I noticed a woman standing at the opening of the ropes course. Her head was in her hands, and she was quietly crying. Then she turned to the counselor standing next to her and said, "When you told me he would do camp, I didn't believe you. He can do anything here. I didn't believe it. I just can't believe this." The counselor put her hand on the mother's shoulder, and they stood there together smiling and crying.

My children and I have never forgotten that moment. We were able to see a camper show great courage, staffers provide support with their training and equipment, and caregivers cry tears of joy and pain mixed together. We felt so privileged to be part of a camp that champions all young people to have the best week of their lives.

We all play different roles when it comes to advocacy. No one person is asked to do everything, but we are all required to do something. My hope is that this story helps you understand the different roles that are required in this work of championing. Some of us need to start cheering more loudly, some of us need to use our expertise to make the impossible possible, and some of us need to stand with others and be willing to smile and cry as we encourage them on their journey. May we see each challenge as an opportunity for advocacy and empathy.

This is the kingdom of heaven: adjusting our spaces and making room for everyone, bearing one another's burdens for the glory of the Lord, and endlessly devoting our time and attention to others so each person God created will have the best possible life on earth. Advocacy and empathy go hand in hand because both are needed to maneuver through life's obstacles and humbly take on challenges that test us and strengthen us.

May we respond to Jen's words and become champions for those we love and will learn to love by the grace of God.

Committed to learning,
Jamie Collins, PhD

Introduction

$\mathcal{E}$arly one Friday morning, I sat quietly with my knees tucked under the horseshoe table by the door in my four-year-old daughter's classroom. I had arrived a few minutes early, a bit disheveled from the morning rush of getting out the door. Coffee in hand, I looked around the classroom. Between sips, I couldn't help but smile. Brightly colored posters and bulletin boards covered every wall. Shelves full of picture books, puzzles, and buckets held all sorts of classroom treasures.

With my mom-sized body folded into a child-sized chair, I was ready for the routine parent-teacher meeting with Charlie's teachers. Several weeks ago, I had scheduled a twenty-minute slot with her teachers. I was one of several parents with whom the teachers would meet that morning. This was a meeting that felt both familiar to me and very different at the same time: familiar because it was the kind of meeting I had held a hundred times as an elementary school teacher in the same town only a few years earlier, but different because, this time, I sat on the other side of the table. My sips of coffee did little to calm my nerves.

As I waited for the meeting to begin, I wondered if my daughter had sat in this very same chair during small group time with her classmates and teachers. Maybe Charlie gathered here with her reading group each day, receiving instruction and engaging in daily activities. Or perhaps this was where Charlie worked on puzzles or practiced cutting with scissors, activities she struggled with due to her lack of fine motor skills. Or maybe this was where she ate lunch each day, sitting next to her friends and enjoying food served on a brightly colored cafeteria tray. Knowing Charlie, the vegetables in that partitioned tray would remain untouched, while the section holding the "hot potatoes" (Charlie's name for mashed potatoes) would be scraped clean. My wandering mind reengaged as the teachers made their preparations on the other side of the table.

Charlie's teachers were busy organizing a collection of yellow folders, various worksheets, and reports. After sorting the pile of papers, one teacher gently slid them to my side of the table. Uncomfortable silence transitioned into lighthearted small talk as we briefly discussed the weather and our weekend plans. That friendly beginning gave me no indication of what this parent-teacher meeting was about to become.

Before sitting on *this* side of the table, I sat on *that* side of the table. *That* side of the table represented my life before motherhood, a life filled with students and homework and assessments of all kinds. In that life I delivered the updates on student progress and discussed their behavior in the classroom. I was the one who shifted folders and sorted papers and evaluations. I explained the assessment tools that demonstrated students' progress. I was the one who shared information with parents and let them know how their child was performing that year. It was my job and my joy, and I think of and miss it often.

But now, on *this* side, I suddenly realized that these meetings feel much different when you're the parent. Papers are not just papers but are, in a way, a reflection of who your child is and what they are becoming. On *this* side, it's not just a routine twenty-minute time slot. For a parent raising a child with special needs, it's a recurring reality check as your child's atypical abilities are compared to a typical child their age.

But this was not my first time to be on *this* side of the table. On *this* side of the table, while Charlie was still in my belly, my doctor asked me, "Do you know much about Down syndrome?" On *this* side of the table, health professionals told me things like, "You have the choice to terminate this pregnancy." On *this* side of the table, the specialist said, "We see two holes in her heart." On *this* side of the table, doctors said, "She will need orthotics her whole life to walk properly."

Ever since Charlotte has been in my life, I have sat on *this* side of the table listening to doctors, therapists, geneticists, specialists, and even well-meaning friends and family. I have heard every possible attempt by people on the other side of the table to lighten the blow of the recent report or test that found something new anchored in my daughter's third copy of her twenty-first chromosome.

Sitting on this side of the table has served as a crash course in parenting a child with special needs. Over the years I have experienced various emotions while hearing reports about my daughter. At times, I am full of courage and confidence. Even when we receive a negative report, we feel grace and remain full of faith. Other times, I feel frustrated. It can be discouraging to hear the same bad news, to hear that your child is still struggling, even though you have done your best to pray and parent. And at times, I hate to admit, I have felt . . . nothing. If I am being honest, sometimes I don't feel hopeful or fearful, just tired—tired of more unknowns, tired of hearing calculated guesses and attempting to temporarily fix the temporary body of my firstborn baby girl.

I scanned the kind faces of the teachers sitting across from me, teachers who worked with Charlie every day and who loved my daughter and invested in her for hours each week. But even their kindness and love for Charlie didn't ease the difficult dialogue. Each folder they slid to my side of the table held a paper that compared Charlie to other kids her age. Those papers showed graphs and data that didn't place Charlie in the "above average," "average," or even the "below average" range for skills and developmental milestones. Charlie's papers showed something very different.

"She just can't . . ."

"She's just not able to . . ."

"She isn't at the level of my other students."

Phrase after phrase flowed across the table as my heart sank lower and lower in the murky waters of someone else's truth about my daughter. I typically maintained a professional, strong-mom face in these moments, but that day the despairing comments built like a wave and knocked me off my feet. Unable to brace myself against its size and strength, the urge to cry slowly rose from my chest to my face, and I felt tears trickle down my cheeks. Like an outgoing tide, every word spoken by the teachers pulled me deeper into despair. I had not planned on this becoming an emotional interaction between me and her teachers, but it was too late. The floodgates opened, and my strong-mom face crumpled. I was devastated.

Even though we had discussed a lot of positive things about Charlie, these negative words, spoken honestly, pierced my momma heart and left me feeling defeated and hopeless.

Words that point out our children's limitations can wound us as parents. These wounds open us up to hopelessness, which can lead to discouragement and eventually defeat. It is in these moments we have a choice: We can choose to give in to defeat, or, as parents whom I believe God has chosen for our children, we can choose to remember the truth that we are not alone. It is in these moments that Jesus is near to our hearts and invites us to respond, not to the pain or the pressures of parenting, but to Himself.

Time and time again, I find myself with the choice to either lie down in defeat or rise up as Jesus extends fresh hope, renewed strength, and glorious grace to move beyond a place of discouragement and into a place where I can once again stand up and be the parent I am called to be.

In my first book, *Chosen for Charlie: When God Gifts You with a Special-Needs Child*, I shared about the calling and power God has bestowed on the parents of children with special needs. We are chosen to love and care for our children. When God got ahold of my heart and told me that I was the mother chosen for Charlie, it healed me. It caused me to have an entirely different perspective of my daughter's diagnosis. That new vision for her life has served as the foundation for the way I live my life as a parent raising a child with special needs. God gifted our family with Charlie. We are privileged to care for her, fight for her, and pray for her. I pray that this truth carries weight in your heart as well and that you will see yourself as chosen for your child who is a precious gift—one worth treasuring and protecting. God has a great purpose for your child and your family, and He is with you every step of the way.

In *Champion for Charlie*, I want to dive deeper into the role for which God has chosen us. When we know what we are chosen for, we will be better able to see the purpose behind the moments of defeat and pain. We will be moved out of the valley and into victory.

Introduction

My friend, God has chosen you to champion for your child. Charlie has Down syndrome, but I wrote this book for anyone who is raising a child with special needs, be it autism, long-term illness, physical delays, cognitive impairments, emotional disorders, or mental health issues. I believe this call to rise up and champion applies to any parent who wishes to advocate for their child with greater purpose and passion. As the champions of our children—special-needs or typical—we must get up and push forward every time the wave of despair knocks us down. We will have hard days. We will be on *this* side of the table throughout our child's life. But the way we choose to respond makes all the difference—for us and for the child who relies on us. Because we know we are chosen to champion, we can rise up!

You were created to overcome.

What power there is in this calling to be a champion for your children! As you lean into God and take hold of His Word, you will walk in His grace, and He will enable you to live with a greater strength and purpose than ever before. You were created to overcome. It's time to see yourself the way God sees you. When you realize that you are chosen to champion, you will rise up and walk in victory, not because your external circumstances have changed but because your internal reality has transformed.

Dear friend, I want you to join me and make the choice to live with greater faith. Don't lie down or live discouraged because you are on *this* side. Let's live as parents who embrace the calling to be the chosen champions for our children!

It's time to walk into your destiny as an overcoming, hope-filled parent and believer. The calling is yours. The invitation is here. Will you accept it?

Chapter 1
An Invitation to Rise Up

*He reached down from on high and took hold of me;
he drew me out of deep waters.*

—Psalm 18:16, NIV

Life can make us weary. It's no secret. No parent is exempt from exhaustion. Whether it's the result of a series of events trickling down—the non-stop schedule, the daily routine, the constant ups and downs—or a tidal wave that takes us out in one fell swoop, parenting has a way of wearing on our minds and our hearts. On our most challenging days, when the sun rises again and we need to face the responsibilities of parenting, there's not enough coffee in the world to revive us from the kind of weariness that makes us want to roll over, pull the covers over our head, and hide a bit longer from the day that awaits.

My husband, Luke, and I have been raising a child with special needs alongside our other two children for nine years now. From the prenatal tests revealing the possibility of Trisomy 21 followed by the blood tests confirming our daughter's genetic abnormality, we have been on a journey with Charlie as we've learned how to parent, discipline, advocate for, and nurture a child with special needs. We have walked through the doors of doctors' offices, hospitals, emergency rooms, specialists, and therapy centers. We have endured countless tests, doctor visits, annual IEPs (Individualized Education Plan) for school, and on-again, off-again therapies. We have had overnight stays in hospitals and clinics and slept in cold, dark rooms between white sheets while listening to the steady beeping of breathing machines and heart monitors. We have received medical bills beyond our bank account balance and completed mountains of paperwork in hopes of finding financial assistance. We have had to learn and grow as parents as we've overcome obstacles in communicating with our daughter, teaching her self-awareness, and encouraging social acceptance among peers.

> *If you find yourself feeling weary and wanting to throw in the towel, you are not alone.*

I share all this with you not to receive pity, but to connect with you. I know that you may have had similar experiences as a parent of a child with special needs. I realize, too, that your list of responsibilities and challenges may far exceed anything Luke and I have walked through thus far. Even if our circumstances are different, the thing we have in common is the risks that exist in these circumstances: the risk to become weary; the risk to feel discouraged and overwhelmed; the risk to give up, give in, and join the party—the pity party. (I've done my fair share of partying with this crowd—at times, I've even been the ringleader.)

My friend, if you find yourself feeling weary and wanting to throw in the towel, you are not alone, and you have the right book in your hands.

Reset Required

When I need to unwind or de-stress, running usually does the trick for me. I like to think of it as a way to reset. A run helps clear my head and relieve the stress that builds up throughout the day from ordinary tasks, like paying the bills, watching the laundry pile up again, managing the kids, and taking care of our home. Not long ago, I was on a run when I realized that I needed much more than a reset—I needed a rescue.

It was March 2020. The COVID pandemic was sweeping across the globe. Life was changing rapidly. Businesses were closing their doors, cities and towns were shutting down, and we had all received the message to stay home. The phrases "social distancing" and "new normal" became part of our everyday vocabulary. And every time I turned on the news, coverage on the pandemic flashed across the screen.

Amid all the changes, the thing that rocked my small world in southeast Michigan was a call from the school. Like many other parents who have a child with special needs, I felt more than a little overwhelmed when I got the call letting me know that schools were closed and students would stay home for an indeterminate amount of time.

I'm sure kids across the nation rejoiced at the news that they were on an extra-long spring break. For us, however, school is an essential part of life. Charlotte thrives on structure. She needs the support of an expert team of teachers and her weekly therapies. She counts on going to her classroom—a setting designed for her to succeed—every weekday. All of that vanished with a single phone call.

A rush of worries overwhelmed me: *Is this for real? How am I going to do this? I'm not cut out for this. There is no way I can juggle all three kids and give Charlotte the instruction and support she needs. I'm not gonna make it!*

My remedy? A run. I needed to get out of the house. I needed some time to gather my thoughts. With each step, I hoped to find an escape, as if I could run from the pandemic and the loss of all things normal. I somehow believed each stride might move me one step closer to peace.

My feet pounded the paved streets of my little—and suddenly quiet—town. I ran past empty historic buildings and "Sorry, we're closed" signs on restaurant doors. My feet moved quickly, but not as fast as my racing mind. The weight of the current circumstances grew heavier with every turn.

I know how to be a mom to Charlie, but how can I be her teacher too? With my four- and two-year-old in the house, how can I give her the attention she needs? How can I help her make progress? I don't think

I can keep the house running. I don't think I can teach Charlotte. God, I can't do this! I don't want to do this!

Panic set in, and all of my emotions rose inside my chest. My routine run turned into a frantic search for a place where I could have a meltdown. Everywhere I turned, there seemed to be other walkers, runners, and bikers. My secret meltdown would not be secret for long. Then I realized that if I could hold it in a bit longer, I could make it back to my house. So I ran home.

I hit the front door and immediately ran up the stairs, through my bedroom, and into the one place I could find a moment's privacy from the little eyes and little hands that needed me. We all have our secret places of survival—mine happens to be the bathroom. (I'm sure I'm not alone in discovering this safe haven.)

I sunk to the cold tile floor just as the floodgates opened. I cried. I prayed. In that moment, I felt all the stress, all the fear, all the weight of worry piled on me at once. It was too much to bear. I just wanted to lie there on the bathroom floor and have my pity party.

Was I being dramatic? Probably.

Was I being rational and reasonable? Not at all. Swept up in my emotions, I saw all the pieces of my life tumbling like dominoes out of their proper place.

My pity party didn't last long, though, because someone else showed up—someone who halted my hopelessness and brought a much-needed reset. Someone who called me to rise up.

Self-Check

Have you ever had one of those moments when you felt like the world was crashing in on you? In that moment, you feel like giving up and giving in to that weariness. Caring for a child with special needs adds an extra layer of fatigue to the already tiring job of parenting. And it's no wonder we're tired! We fight battles daily for the best doctors, best teachers, and best programs. We are constantly on the offense and defense for our children, taking on battles they can't fight for themselves. And as parents who are trying to make a great life for our kids, we can work ourselves into exhaustion until we hit a wall—or a cold tile floor.

Too often, we go and help and fight without stopping to assess our condition. We are so aware of our children—how they are doing and what they need—but we neglect to look inward. So before we go any further, let's pause and do a self-check on where you are right now:

- What condition do you find yourself in?
- Are you weary?
- Are you feeling discouraged?
- Have you hit a wall that you just can't seem to break through?
- Are you running and running in search of answers or peace?
- Are you hiding out in a secret place, considering giving up?

Maybe you are where I was, feeling overwhelmed, lying on the bathroom floor, and wishing you could run from the world around you. If that's the case, I want you to know you are not alone. There is a Savior who is always near. If you choose to call out to Him in those moments, He will hear you. And He always has the answer to whatever crisis you are facing.

In the book of Psalms, David, someone God describes as "a man after his own heart" (1 Samuel 13:14, ESV), remembers the faithfulness of God when he was faced with opposition and pain: "On the day I called, you answered me" (Psalm 138:3, ESV).

God hears us when we call, and He has the answer we need in our moments of pain, discouragement, fear, and loneliness. He comes to our side ready to respond with His love and strength.

Recognize Your Reality

One of the inspirations for this book is the story of a man in great need of a breakthrough. He desperately needed a miracle. He needed Jesus to come into his situation and bring a healing touch.

We find his story in the gospel of John. The Pool of Bethesda was a place where the sick and lame eagerly waited for the waters to stir so they could get in and experience healing. Day after day, this man watched others rise up healed from the waters. But he had not been lucky enough to make it into the water himself. He was yet to have his breakthrough moment. This is the passage that came to my heart as I lay on the bathroom floor:

> *Here a great number of disabled people used to lie—the blind, the lame, the paralyzed. One who was there had been an invalid for thirty-eight years. When Jesus saw him lying there and learned that he had been in this condition for a long time, he asked him, "Do you want to get well?"*
> *"Sir," the invalid replied, "I have no one to help me into the pool when the water is stirred. While I am trying to get in, someone else goes down ahead of me."*
>
> John 5:3–7, NIV

This man who lay by the pool of Bethesda had been sick for thirty-eight years. When I think about this man and his physical condition, it's hard for me to imagine what his life must have been like. In different translations, it says he "had an infirmity" (NKJV), "had been ill" (AMP), or "had been sick" (NLT). We aren't sure what his condition was, but we know he had been in that same condition for almost four decades, and he was ready for a change. He was waiting by that pool, desperately needing a miracle. He was anxious for his healing moment, but he hadn't gotten it just yet. Whenever the waters stirred, everyone else had a chance to get in, but he just couldn't get his timing right.

I'm not sure why his miracle was taking so long. It seems to me he would have seen those waters stirred enough times to get it right sooner than later. But perhaps this man wasn't missing out; perhaps he was being set up for a life-changing, soul-searching, future-transforming moment.

We see from the story that a greater opportunity, a greater gift, was in store for him. Rather than a healing touch from the waters, he would experience the healing touch of a Savior.

Maybe, like this man, you are in great need of a miraculous touch. You are searching for more than a good cup of coffee, a stress-relieving run, or a morning to sleep in a bit longer. Maybe, like me, you find yourself wanting and needing something so much more than a quick fix. You are tired of being tired. Your bad days are outnumbering your good days. You wonder if you really have what it takes to raise this child God has given you.

If you're wondering why I'm starting the book about being a champion for your child with a Bible story, it's because, just like this man who lay by the Pool of Bethesda, we all need the deep work of a Savior. Before we can be our best for our children, we have to recognize whose we are and where our real source of help lies. If we look anywhere other than to the Great Healer in our times of need, we will remain overwhelmed, overburdened, and exhausted.

Roadblocks to Rising Up

When we look at this story of the ill man by the pool of Bethesda, we see a miracle take place, but only after Jesus searched the man's heart. Before telling the sick man to get up, Jesus asked him a question: "Do you want to get well?"

The answer seems obvious. This man had been eagerly waiting in a location where miracles regularly took place. But Jesus didn't take the obvious for granted. He dug into the condition of this man's heart and faith. Do you really want to move from this sickness to a better way of life? Do you want to be different? Do you want to live changed from the inside out? I wonder if Jesus asked this question because he wanted to know if healing was something the sick man really wanted. He thought he wanted it and said he wanted it, but was he truly ready to live transformed?

Rising up and living differently isn't always easy. In my own life, I've experienced roadblocks that have kept me stuck, even though I said I wanted a breakthrough. I might think I am ready for Jesus to touch my life so I can live in a new way, but when He asks me to rise up, I sometimes have a hard time giving up my worry, pain, or stress because I know that living differently will require change on my part. But when I accept His gift of strength and healing, when I choose to live in His peace, I am a better wife, a better mother—a better champion.

I don't want you to miss out on your calling and purpose as a parent because of the pain or stress you might be experiencing. I want to share some roadblocks that I've experienced so you can recognize what might be keeping you from advocating for your children and living in victory.

Roadblock #1: Our Pain Becomes a Part of Us

Pain had become the invalid man's companion. His illness had become his identity. His condition had become a limitation that kept him from living a life full of joy, full of love, full of purpose. Jesus didn't want him to remain sick, and Jesus doesn't want you and me to continue to suffer either.

If you are reading this book, I believe you want to overcome your misery and move forward. If you are like me, you realize life is too short and you aren't meant to live weary, discouraged, or defeated. Every parent has hard days, but God calls us to so much more than a life stuck in despair or overwhelmed by stress. Our kids deserve better.

When pain becomes a part of who we are, we hesitate when Jesus asks, "Do you want to get well?" Suffering may seem like a badge of honor—or it may just feel normal. We may believe that being full of hope and joy isn't the right way to live in light of our circumstances. How can we rise up when our external circumstances haven't changed? How can we rise up while our family members or close friends are still hurting and carrying pain? We may even believe that our pain is what connects us to the people who are struggling alongside of us.

The mindset that allows pain or struggle to become our identity can be a major roadblock to rising up and living differently. Yes, it has been a part of our story, but today our story can turn the page to a new chapter. The pain can be part of the past rather than our present.

The decision to move forward does not mean forgetting what has happened. It does require embracing a new way of relating to the pain and allowing God to do a new work in you—a work you can't do yourself. It is a work that only He can do for you and in you, to heal you and transform you.

I love the passage found in 2 Corinthians where Paul writes to encourage believers that the past can be left behind and we can live in a new way: "Therefore, if anyone is in Christ, he is a new creation. The old has passed away; behold, the new has come" (2 Corinthians 5:17, ESV).

There is transforming power at work in us when we belong to Jesus and have a relationship with Him. He can recreate, resurrect, and restore us in ways beyond our understanding. If you are ready to let go of your weariness and pain, then you can allow Jesus to create a new way of thinking and living that will move you into His purpose and destiny for your life.

Roadblock #2: Misery Loves Company

When we read about this man who was sick and waiting for his breakthrough, we see that he was not alone. He laid by that pool every day surrounded by others who were hurting. As the man sat among this crowd, I imagine he made small talk throughout the day. And if you have ever made small talk with people who are battling an illness or suffering, the mood of the conversation typically isn't hopeful and uplifting. I'm sure there was groaning, complaining, maybe even weeping as they suffered side by side and longed for their miracles. This man felt the weight not only of his own illness but also of the illnesses of others. I'm sure he was thankful to have others by his side who were feeling the same things, thinking the same way, and sharing the same pain.

Have you ever been around a group of people who share a common suffering? It can be comforting to know you are not alone. You exchange stories. You compare battle wounds. There is truth to the saying, "Misery loves company."

When we have painful experiences or feel overwhelmed by life, it feels natural to reach out to others who share the same pain. It's easier than ever with social media at our fingertips to connect through our misery. We can post about a bad day or complain about this or that, and instantly a virtual crowd forms with people sharing comments and images in response to our pain. We receive validation from others who have endured similar experiences or share our opinions. We also receive sympathy that provides a temporary comfort to the pain. There is something that feels good about not feeling so alone in our suffering.

Now, let me say that it can be a healthy thing to reach out to others when we are hurting. We must, however, be intentional about the people we reach out to. Some people will listen to our pain and then add their own, and we end up feeling even worse. Others offer a listening ear and can provide comfort and strength with an encouraging word or even a hug.

I know that when I feel discouraged or overwhelmed, I have a choice: I can find people to lift me up and speak faith to my heart and hope to my soul; or I can find people who will put up with my wallowing, who add to my painful stories with stories of their own, and who let me sink even deeper into my suffering.

As you rise up and live out the reality of who God says you are, others will have the opportunity to rise up with you.

If you are ready to rise up and live differently, you might need to consider leaving some unhealthy relationships behind. As you rise up and live out the reality of who God says you are, others will have the opportunity to rise up with you. When this happens, it's an awesome thing to live side by side in victory with those on a similar parenting journey. But for those who continue to choose misery and to live untouched and unhealed, your best course of action is to pray for them as you move forward without them. It may be that they would rather remain in their familiar pain because doing so doesn't require a response of faith and action.

Roadblock #3: Suffering Brings Sympathy

I imagine there were people who brought the suffering man food from time to time. Someone must have made sure he had water to drink. Even in his terrible circumstance, there must have been at least a few people who helped take care of him. Perhaps Jesus asked the lame man if he wanted to get well because he wanted the man to recognize the change it would bring in how others treated him. Maybe the man liked the sympathy his sickness brought into his life.

Sympathy can be a sweet thing to have in the midst of our pain.

Our three children seem to be at the peak of their curiosity regarding pretty much everything. They are constantly running and exploring the great outdoors every chance they get. We own a home on a larger piece of property with trees to climb and wooded areas to venture into. My six-year-old often says he is "going on a hike," which means walking straight into a shrub and weaving his body through narrow spaces between branches and twigs. His younger sister follows after him, and she always seems to come back with holes in her pants and her hair tossed about.

I often watch their adventures unfold as I stand on our back deck. As the "hikers" journey through the bushes and trees, it's never too long before I hear a holler followed by frantic footsteps and a panicked "Mom!" I rush to the scene as little hands point to the fresh scrape or cut. More often than not, I don't see the injury at first glance. I have to look, search, and check again. Most of the time, their cry for Mom is less about the injury and more about the sympathy needed in the moment. After a few "poor babies," a cuddle, and kiss on the boo-boo, the kids are back in action continuing with their hike as planned.

Just like children, we can find great comfort and satisfaction in the sympathy and attention we receive from others in life's painful moments. Years ago, I had some major health issues that called for extended stays at the hospital. I became accustomed to the 24/7 care I received from nurses and doctors. While in the hospital room, nurses checked on me and administered pain medication. The hospital staff brought me meals and cleaned up after me. Visitors brought me cards and thoughtful gifts to lift my spirits. The care and sympathy were a great comfort on my road to recovery.

Once I was discharged and back home, I realized I was missing something as I lay on my living room sofa with my crackers and 7UP. I missed the attention. I missed the sympathy. I missed the constant care and attention.

This can happen to us when we move from a state of pain to recovery. We miss the attention our pain brought us, and we can end up wanting to keep the pain and the attention that comes with it. This is a trap. We must acknowledge it as a roadblock that keeps us from rising up, overcoming, and moving forward.

As you consider these three roadblocks, ask yourself the question Jesus asked the sick man: "Do you want to get well?" Has your pain become a part of your identity and a normal part of your parenting? Have you enjoyed the company that misery has brought into your life? Is there a part of you that enjoys the sympathy it brings? My friend, are you really ready for a breakthrough? If you choose to move past these roadblocks, Jesus is ready to help you rise up!

Get Honest

As we prepare to rise up, we have to get honest with ourselves. What do you think the lame man thought when Jesus asked, "Do you want to get well?" The man might have been thinking, *Really, Jesus, do you think I like being in this condition? Do you think I want to lay here day after day, unchanged, damaged, and left to fend for myself?*

Jesus was looking at the state of this man's heart, and He's looking at your heart and my heart today as well.

When I look back on my darkest seasons of discouragement or pain, I find that even though I wanted to be made whole, parts of me weren't as ready to let go of the "illness" as Jesus was ready to heal me and move me forward. I am challenged to answer Jesus' question, "Do I want to get well?" with all honesty. To be honest, Jesus, my condition has become a part of me. This pain connects me to other people I care about. The sickness I carry causes others to give me sympathy and attention I desire. To be healed would mean I have to do things differently, and I don't know if I'm ready for that change.

Just like Jesus searched the lame man's heart, He is asking us each today the same question: "Do you want to get well?" That question could be asked in other ways:

- Do you really want this?
- Do you want to move beyond your current condition?
- Do you really want to live differently, even if it requires more of you?
- Do you want to live a life of overcoming?
- Do you want to have a testimony of healing, or do you choose to carry your hurt day after day?"

I hope your answer to these questions is a loud and resounding, "I want to be made well! I don't want to live like this anymore!" He is more than able, but you have to accept His healing.

If yes is your answer today, then you are ready to rise up! You can be made well! You can live an overcoming life as a parent championing for your child! You can rise above that which has overwhelmed you as a parent. As you respond to Jesus in this moment of invitation, He will come and bring the change you need to be the parent He has called you to be.

Humility Leads to Healing

As we respond to Jesus and His invitation to rise up, we can embrace His healing once we recognize our need for Him. When we come, fully realizing and admitting our limitations as parents, Jesus will respond to our prayer and our honest pursuit of Him. To be honest and humble before Jesus prepares the way for His healing touch in our lives.

What does a humble prayer sound like? Well, just two simple words can pave the way for a humble heart to encounter Jesus: *I can't*. We must get to a place of total dependence on Christ and admit that we can't do life without Him. The world tries to convince us to believe I can. I can do it all and be it all for my family and children. I can juggle work, the household, the finances, the weekly schedule—I can do it all. But the truth of the Gospel is that we can't do anything apart from Christ (Acts 17:28). We can't heal ourselves, and we can't take care of all our family's needs.

There is so much freedom in *I can't*. This isn't negative thinking; this is a humility of heart that is paving the way for the promises and faithfulness of God to be demonstrated in your life! *I can't* enables the I AM to come in and bring a supernatural supply of grace and strength. *I can't* should be a part of our daily prayer life. *I can't make it today without You, God. I can't find peace apart from You. I can't raise these kids on my own. I can't make this decision unless You give me wisdom. I can't control the future, but everything is in Your hands. I can't find healing or wholeness apart from You.*

In Christ, all things are possible (Luke 1:37). In Him is life and wholeness (Psalm 36:9). God created me with the need for a Savior. He knows I can't. My admission of *I can't* opens the door for His power to be at work in and through me. In my humility and recognition of my weakness, I encounter Jesus, and my heart finds healing and purpose.

Let's conclude this chapter with a final prayer together as we respond to the invitation to rise up:

Jesus, today I want to be made well. I can't do this life on my own. As You give me the opportunity to rise up and overcome, I want to walk in Your victory and be made whole—in mind, body, and spirit—so that my life can be a testimony of Your power. Thank You that I am healed and that I can walk in Your victory each day. My victory is not based on my feelings or circumstances, but on the power of Christ at work in me to raise me up and set my feet on a firm foundation. Today, I will rise up and walk in victory. In Jesus' name, amen.

Chapter 2
Rise Up. Now What?

Jesus told him, "Stand up, pick up your mat, and walk!"

—John 5:8, NLT

You have answered the call to rise up. Jesus has given you the opportunity to step into something new, and you have taken it. Now what? What does this mean? How should you feel? What if, after your Jesus encounter, you still feel the same?

Well, my friend, sometimes we respond to the invitation to rise up and feel a glorious rush of emotions that launches us into victory. More often than not, however, the rising up is less about feelings and more about the choices that follow—the deliberate decisions we make every day, several times a day, to rise up and live the overcoming life of a parent called to champion for their child. Rising up is a resolve to no longer lie down, be stuck, or live with a defeated spirit. We now have the opportunity to live out our healing moment. It's time to "pick up your mat and walk."

Starting Line

There is nothing like the starting line at a race. Whether it's a marathon with thousands of runners or a schoolyard race against your classmates, standing at the starting line sparks a thrill of excitement. You know a new challenge is ahead and something special is about to begin. The pre-race jitters and fellow runners wait for you on that line.

You feel a sense of pride because you decided to show up, participate, run your heart out, and make it across the finish line.

At every race there are runners and spectators. When you choose to rise up and move to the starting line as a parent, you choose the position of action. Rather than sitting on the sidelines and watching other parents champion and cheer for their children, you have your feet in a position that will create motion and forward momentum. You are choosing to rise up for your child. You are choosing to participate in the race.

I know that as you stand at this starting line, you have high hopes to accomplish something great. Maybe you are competitive—you race to win. Maybe you're only competing with yourself and hoping to beat your last race time. Either way, I am excited to be at this starting line with you.

Many runners have gone before us—parents who have chosen to rise up and make a profound impact. These amazing mothers, fathers, grandmas, and grandpas stood up with faith, prayed bold prayers, and blazed the trail on which we now run. They have shaped the opportunities our children now have.

Change happens when champion parents show up on race day, and let me say, this is a race in which I am honored to participate. Blessed to be chosen to be in this race, you and I stand at the starting line not because we have to, but because we get to. We get to run. We get to follow in the footsteps of heroes who ran this race long before we stepped up to the line.

Yes, some runners may have gotten weary trying to run alone. Exhausted, they withdrew from the race and sat down on the sidelines in personal defeat. Maybe you have witnessed those runners—those parents and families who just couldn't rise up under the weight of the calling to run the race before them. But you and I are choosing to rise up and run—not in our own power, but with the knowledge that He can even when we can't.

As we run, we cling to a promise of the Lord. The Word of God says, "But those who hope in the LORD will renew their strength. They will soar on wings like eagles; they will run and not grow weary, they will walk and not be faint" (Isaiah 40:31, NIV).

I ran marathons for years. I ran across Oklahoma City, Little Rock, Chicago, Detroit, and the Sleepy Bears Dunes of Michigan. I never ran a marathon expecting to come in first place, but I always came ready to give it my all. And every time, I had the strength to cross the finish line. As we champion for our children, God will give us the strength to complete our race as well.

As we run together, let us not compare ourselves to those running alongside us. In this race, it does not matter who is stronger or faster. What matters is that we each give it our all as we fight for what matters: our children.

Welcome to the starting line. Let's do this race together!

Rising Up Is a Response

Sometimes rising up and moving forward is easier said than done. We make the decision to be a champion for our children and step up to the starting line, but then we start to second-guess ourselves. Our feelings can cause us to doubt God's promises and the newfound strength and hope we have as Christ's power works in us.

> *Above all else, guard your heart, for everything you do flows from it.*
>
> *—Proverbs 4:23, NIV*

Rising up is a choice to live according to God's promises for your family. It is both a physical action and a mindset of overcoming negative and hopeless thinking. I find that I continually have to guard my mind and resist thoughts that pull me back down. To finish this race with excellence, I must anchor my heart and mind in the truth. I have to hold on to what God says about my child and who I am as a parent.

It's easy to get discouraged when I focus on the negative. Holding on to God's promises requires daily effort, especially when I look at Charlie and hear the whisper of negative thoughts like, *Charlie isn't making progress. Charlie isn't where I thought she would be. Charlie seems to be taking steps backward. I just don't know how to help her. Am I doing the right things? She would be making more progress if I was doing this or that. I'm not as good of a mom as so-and-so.*

Can you relate? Those negative, uninvited thoughts creep in, and before we know it, we have spiraled down into a pit of discouragement, convinced that we are terrible parents and our child isn't going to succeed in life.

In those moments, we have the choice either to wallow or to remind ourselves that we have been called to rise up and live in God's strength. If you are like me, you need this reminder daily. We are in this race together, running with Jesus as our guide and healer, and that truth is what empowers us to live in victory despite the challenges we face with our children.

> *Do you not know that in a race all the runners run, but only one gets the prize? Run in such a way as to get the prize.*
> —1 Corinthians 9:24, NIV

Affirmed with the truth, then, our response must be to give this race our all. We can't live half-hearted. We need to be fully committed to our children and the calling on our lives. Like the Apostle Paul, we must run the race like champions who want to win for our children's sake.

Holding On to the Promises

Overcoming negative thoughts is a battle we will have to face every day. Fears about our children, concerns for the future, problems that need to be solved—all these thoughts flood our minds and can push us right back where we started, before we stood at the starting line.

God warns us to guard our way of thinking and what we focus on. 2 Corinthians 10:5 tells us to take every thought captive and make it line up with the truth of what God says in His Word. Being aware and alert to the thoughts running through our minds, casting out the lies, and taking hold of the truth takes work!

I keep several scriptures close to my heart for the purpose of guarding my mind. When I worry about Charlie, I simply remind myself of what God's Word says about her.

- Charlie will grow in wisdom and stature and favor with You and man. (Luke 2:52)
- God, Your plans for Charlie are good. (Jeremiah 29:11)

- Charlie will be like a tree planted by rivers of water, bearing fruit in every season, not withering but prospering. (Psalm 1:3)
- Charlie's life was created for Your glory to be revealed. (John 9:3)
- Charlie can do this because all things are possible with You. (Matthew 19:26)
- God, You will equip me and give me wisdom as a parent. (2 Timothy 2:21)

These are some of the promises I hold on to for Charlie, and I encourage you to believe them for your child as well. We can champion best when our minds are set on the promises and truths God has given us about our children.

In the Desert

I want to share with you a powerful story from Genesis 21 about a mother named Hagar. She was the handmaiden to Sarah, Abraham's wife. God had promised that Abraham would be the father of many nations and have more descendants than anyone could count. Sarah and Abraham were eager to have a child and see God's promise fulfilled. After years of waiting, however, they took matters into their own hands.

Sarah tried to make God's promise happen, but it wasn't the way God intended. Sarah asked Abraham to lay with Hagar, her handmaiden. Soon Hagar became pregnant and had a son. What seemed to be the solution for fulfilling God's promise became a problem for Hagar, Abraham, and Sarah.

The birth of Hagar's son didn't bring joy, but tension and stress in the household. Sound familiar? Maybe the birth of your child and the diagnosis that came with them caused tension and stress in your home. It certainly did in our home. Luke and I were excited about welcoming a new baby girl into our lives, but her diagnosis brought a whole new level of stress and worry as well, the kind of heartbreak we never expected to experience as parents. We mourned the future our daughter might never have. We worried about imminent health challenges.

With heavy hearts and tough conversations, we worked through the new reality for our family.

The tension grew between Sarah and Hagar, so much so that Sarah demanded Hagar be sent away to the desert.

> *Early the next morning Abraham took some food and a skin of water and gave them to Hagar. He set them on her shoulders and then sent her off with the boy. She went on her way and wandered in the Desert of Beersheba.*
>
> —*Genesis 21:14, NIV*

Hagar was now a wandering mother. Alone with her son in the desert, she was uncertain of what lay ahead for this new life she had not anticipated or asked for.

I relate to Hagar in several ways: She was a parent who felt overwhelmed and lost in unfamiliar territory. Wandering in the desert, I'm sure she had difficulty imagining life turning out well for herself and her son.

My heart breaks for Hagar as I imagine the loneliness she must have felt. She had to be strong enough for her son to keep moving forward, forcing herself to take one step after another as they journeyed into the unknown. I imagine her carrying him, talking to him, and trying to keep his spirits up. As she grows more and more weary, she hits a breaking point.

> *When the water in the skin was gone, she put the boy under one of the bushes. Then she went off and sat down about a bowshot away, for she thought, "I cannot watch the boy die." And as she sat there, she began to sob.*
>
> —*Genesis 21:15-16, NIV*

The circumstances had become too much for this mother. Life and its stresses caused Hagar to feel beaten and overwhelmed, and she was ready to give up. She had run out of resources. She had nothing left to give her child, let alone herself. She just wanted to sit down and pull herself out of the race.

While raising a child with special needs, we may find ourselves feeling like Hagar. Wandering alone, trying to make the most of our desert, we feel like we have explored every option. We have made the phone calls to doctors. We have filled out the paperwork. We have read the right books. We have created the right systems and schedules for our child to succeed. We have completed the recommended therapy sessions. We have done the extra tutoring. And still, here we are in this desert. We have exhausted our resources. We have worn ourselves thin. We are tired, and we just need to sit down and have a moment to grieve and rest.

Go to Him

In that precious moment of honesty and vulnerability, God saw Hagar and her son. He extended His mercy and compassion to her in a personal and practical way. Let's keep reading and find out what happened to Hagar.

> *God heard the boy crying, and the angel of God called to Hagar from heaven and said to her, "What is the matter, Hagar? Do not be afraid; God has heard the boy crying as he lies there. Lift the boy up and take him by the hand, for I will make him into a great nation."*
>
> —*Genesis 21:17–18, NIV*

What did God tell Hagar to do? He instructed her to go to her son, lift him up, and grab him by the hand. Hagar has a rising up moment, and her first step is toward her son.

As we learn from Hagar's story, our first step when we have chosen to rise up from our defeat and into our destiny is to go to our children. That means pushing aside our feelings and the battles raging within us and simply going to the child who needs us. Our focus shifts from our circumstance to our child and their need for a champion.

When I feel exhausted and overwhelmed by the responsibility of parenting Charlie, sometimes I find respite simply by stopping for a moment and just being with her. Whether it's finding her in her room and giving her a hug, taking her on a walk, or sitting beside her on the couch, I go to Charlie and tell her, "Honey, I love you. I am so proud of you. You are such a good sister. You are so beautiful. I love your hair and your beautiful eyes. You are so special to Mommy. Daddy and I love you so much." I rise up and go to her.

When we go to our children and focus on who they are and what they need in that moment, our thoughts shift from ourselves to them and the work of God that must continue in their lives and in our family's life. Hagar needed to go to her son, and we need to go to our children.

After Hagar goes to her son, it says that she lifted him up. What does it mean to "lift up" our children? I believe that if I am going to lift up Charlie, I need to stop talking about the problem and focus on her as a person. I celebrate who she is and what she can do. I don't look at the desert of my circumstances, but I choose to look at Charlie. I choose to focus on her. In doing so, my calling to champion and care for her is once again refocused, renewed, and restored. My perspective shifts from pity to purpose. My purpose as her mother is to care for her.

The story of Hagar can be a warning to us not to give in to the temptation to sit down and give up on our children. Our purpose is to rise up because God has a plan, even in the desert, and a purpose for our child's life.

God had great plans for Hagar and her son. He wanted to make Hagar's son into a great nation. If she had given in to defeat in the desert, she never would have seen him become what God had promised. I believe God has a great plan for our children, and it's one beyond our understanding. It's bigger than a bad day in a dry desert, and it is worth rising up for.

Our purpose is to rise up because God has a plan, even in the desert, and a purpose for our child's life.

Then Comes the Provision

Something incredible happened when Hagar chose to take her eyes off herself and go to her son. When she rose up and went to her child, she found provision!

> *Then God opened her eyes and she saw a well of water. So she went and filled the skin with water and gave the boy a drink. God was with the boy as he grew up. He lived in the desert and became an archer. While he was living in the Desert of Paran, his mother got a wife for him from Egypt.*
>
> —Genesis 21:19–21, NIV

When Hagar rose up in obedience, God opened her eyes to the miracle that He had provided for her. God supplied water for her and her son in the desert, which was exactly what they needed in that moment.

When we choose to rise up and go to our children, God offers provision: He gives us the hope, strength, and wisdom we need to care for them. Sometimes He provides water in the desert, and sometimes He puts just the right people in our path, people who can help us overcome our present circumstance and move toward the promise God has for our child.

What an incredible lesson we can learn from Hagar. Although her circumstance had overwhelmed her, she chose to rise up in obedience and go to her son, where she found immediate provision and, ultimately, God's fulfillment of His promise to make her child a great nation.

Don't Doubt the Work

I have found that when I make the decision to rise up, the outcome is not always smiles and smooth sailing to sweet victory. Doubt often competes against my newfound hope in the promise and work of God. That doubt causes me to second-guess God and myself. It comes to steal my purpose and tempts me to step back from the starting line and sit down on the sidelines.

As with the soil in the parable of the farmer in Mark 4:13–20, I have to examine the condition of my faith as God speaks a new word (drops a new seed) into my heart. In the parable, the different areas where the seed fell determined what kind of crop—if any—the seed would yield. Some seed fell on ground that was hard and never accepted the seed. Some fell on ground that was shallow and rocky—it wanted the seed but didn't have the ability to accept and nourish it. Some fell on ground that was so thick with weeds that there wasn't room for the seed to grow. But the good soil fully accepted the seed and allowed it to take root and spring up with no hindrances.

I find myself somewhere in between the good soil and the rocky, weed-infested soil. I want to accept the seed with joy, but the doubts and pressures of life keep the seed from fully taking root and springing up to bring new life.

My best, and truly only, defense against doubt and worry is prayer. I pray and remind myself of who God is and what He is doing. *God, You have called me to rise up, so today I rise up. I am not overcome. I am not defeated. I am called to live according to Your word and Your ways. I will rise up and walk in faith, not feelings.*

The enemy wants to distract us. He wants us to believe his lie that God never called us to rise up so we will remain stuck in defeat. When we have a bad day, or when feelings of hopelessness and discouragement begin to chase us down, the enemy instantly causes us to question what God is doing in our lives.

Friend, let me just say, it's okay to have a bad day. We all have those moments when we feel like we are taking steps backward. Fear and worry can pull us into an old way of thinking. Let me encourage you in those moments to take those thoughts captive. Remind yourself of the healing power of Jesus that is at work in your life. Go to God in prayer and lay down those thoughts and emotions. Don't shove them down but acknowledge them. Share your concerns with a trusted, uplifting friend, and ask for prayer.

In this lifelong race, we will have moments when we get tired, and that is to be expected. Good runners don't ignore their bodies when they start to feel weary—they look for the cause. If it's hydration they need, they stop and grab that drink of Powerade so they can keep going. If a muscle starts to cramp, they slow down and walk for a bit. They may even take a short break to do some stretches, remove extra layers that have become too hot, or bend down and tie their shoe.

If you are weary, it's okay to pause and catch your breath. As parents, there will be times when we recognize that hesitation is creeping in, and we need to talk with someone and ask for prayer. We need to deal with the doubt, then get back in the race. Pausing to make an adjustment doesn't mean you're out of the race. Fix what needs fixing, get back in there, and keep running!

If you are weary, it's okay to pause and catch your breath.

Many of us will have lapses in our enthusiasm for championing, which is why we must guard our hearts and minds, take our thoughts captive, and constantly refocus on the truth that God is at work in our lives. God is the author and perfector of our faith (Hebrews 12:2). Having a bad day does not mean our story is taking a U-turn, nor does it mean that God has left us to run alone.

Stay the course, make the necessary adjustments, and on those bad days, remind yourself of who God is, what He has done, and what He is doing in your life. Lean on Him. Surrender to Him rather than to the lies of the enemy. God is bigger and stronger than anything Satan might use to distract or discourage us with.

Truth Keeps Us
On the days when our feelings get us down, we need the truth of God's Word to keep us running on course. Here are some great scriptures to encourage you when rising up and racing forward gets challenging:

"In this world you will have trouble. But take heart! I have overcome the world."

—*John 16:33, NIV*

And we know that in all things God works for the good of those who love him, who have been called according to his purpose.

—*Romans 8:28, NIV*

I can do all things through Christ who strengthens me.

—*Philippians 4:13, NKJV*

Hold on to the promises in these scriptures. I encourage you to write them down along with any others that encourage you. Put them on a note card and post it on your bathroom mirror, on the dashboard of your car, or above your kitchen sink. Get these truths in front of you. There are plenty of opportunities throughout the day to get discouraged, frustrated, or overwhelmed. Rely on God's truth to bring strength and hope in those difficult moments. It's up to us to keep God's Word as the foundation of what we think and believe for our children and the future.

Carry Your Mat

In the previous chapter, we looked at the sick man who lay by the Pool of Bethesda. Like Hagar, he had a "rise up" moment followed by a *Now what?* instruction. The instruction Jesus gave this man is meaningful and applicable for us today as well.

After Jesus had healed the man, He told him what to do next: He told him to pick up his mat and walk. Jesus wanted the man to take his mat with him.

That mat was part of his story. I believe it served as a reminder of what he had overcome. He had encountered and been miraculously healed by Jesus. The mat was his testimony, the physical thing he could point to and tell his story. Jesus wanted him to share his story with others.

You, too, have a mat. You have a story. As you choose each day to rise up, life will meet you with challenges. But as you go to your child and push through feelings that tempt you to doubt the work God is doing, the story you share can impact others' lives. Your response to Jesus empowers you to live as a champion, and your example will inspire others to do the same!

As the sick man shared his story with others, he was not the main character. He wasn't the focal point, Jesus was. The same can and should be true of the stories we share about our families. Jesus is the focus. He is the main character, author, illustrator, publisher, and editor.

As you share your story, keep God as the main focus. He's the only reason you are able to carry your mat in the first place. Let your life bring attention and glory to the One who called you to rise up. Let your life point others to Jesus.

Carry your story with you. Carry it where God has sent you and where He leads you. As we parent, we will have opportunities to share our stories, and in doing so make a difference for our children and for other families who are on a similar journey. Know that as you carry your story and share it with others, you will be strengthened as well. Sharing your story will enable you to keep running. Revelation 12:11 says, "And they have conquered him (the enemy) by the blood of the Lamb and by the word of their testimony..." (ESV, parenthesis added). We have overcome by the blood of the Lamb and the word of our testimony. It's through sharing our story—carrying our mat for all to see—that we can stay on course and find ultimate victory. The enemy wants us to forget what God has done for us. How easy it is to experience a miracle and quickly forget just how amazing God is. Let's declare His goodness together. Let's stay in this race, go to our children, push back the doubt, carry our mats, and move forward as champions.

Chapter 3
Rise Up for What?

And we know that in all things God works for the good of those who love him, who have been called according to his purpose.

—Romans 8:28, NIV

Remember the story of Hagar and what God had planned for her son? God wanted to make him into a great nation. He had given him skills as an archer and even provided a wife for him. Just as God had a great plan for Hagar's son, He has a great plan for our children as well.

God told Hagar to rise up and take the child by his hand. Go to him, be there for him, be his champion. But God didn't stop there. He had a promise for the child whose birth had created so much tension and stress. Had God not beaten Hagar to the punch, she might have asked, "Rise up? For what? Why?"

And maybe you're asking that same question: Rise up for what? What is our reason for rising up? What is our motivation? The answer to that question isn't a what but a who. Who is our motivation? The motivation for rising up is that sweet gift with whom God has entrusted you. For me, it is Charlie, and for you, it is your child.

Rise Up to Champion

When I discovered we would be raising a child with special needs, one word quickly became a part of who I am and my calling as a mother.

It's a word that never carried much weight until I had Charlotte. That word, which now carries so much significance to me, is *advocate*.

Within the world of special needs, we see and hear this word often. Understanding the meaning of this word helps us clarify how to advocate in the best way possible. Synonyms for advocate include protector, supporter, upholder, backer, and my favorite—*champion*. This list of words inspires me as a parent. I want to be a champion not only for Charlie but for all of my children as well. I want to be a mother who protects and supports them in every way possible.

An advocate is also a person who represents someone or something as a spokesman, a crusader, or a campaigner. Yes, yes, and yes to all three! I want to be a spokesperson, a crusader, and a campaigner for my daughter!

Too many times, however, we can get focused on the wrong thing as we try to advocate for our children. Rather than fighting *for* our children, we make the mistake of fighting *against* someone or something. Rather than focusing on our children, we can become focused on the opposition.

> *I want to be a spokesperson, a crusader, and a campaigner for my daughter!*

We saw this play out in the story of Hagar when she and her son were in the desert. She became overwhelmed when she only saw the desert that was fighting against her and her boy. She lost sight of her son and her reason to rise up. God didn't want her to fight the desert (the external circumstances); He wanted her to go to her son, lift him up, take his hand, and get him some water.

As we fight for our children, we need to pick our battles and not allow the external opposition to consume our thoughts and control our feelings. We can't always change the system (school, financial aid, sports programs, etc.), but we can tend to our children and make sure they have what they need to succeed. We can focus on our children and help them thrive in an otherwise challenging environment.

The Power of Approach

I believe how we advocate has a lot to do with our personalities and what's most important to us, as well as our past experiences and the parent advocates we choose to model ourselves after. As parents and caregivers, we all have to find our place in the world of advocacy for our children.

How one parent advocates can look very different from how another advocates. Some parents advocate with an angry heart. They may have endured terrible experiences that left them hurt and feeling as though they aren't fighting for their child but fighting against an unfair system. But rather than taking a position rooted in pain and anger, we can choose a position of peace as we work toward a goal of improving not only the life of our children but the lives of others as well.

To move into a position of successful and life-giving advocacy, we must examine and deal with our hearts. The heart driving the advocate can determine their success. We can advocate better when we have allowed God to heal and strengthen us. When God is our foundation and we are actively seeking His face and being led by Him, we can know our hearts are on the right track. He gives us the reason to champion for our children—the potential and the future He has promised us.

The power is in the approach. Psalm 34:14 emphasizes the importance of peace and doing our best to maintain that peace in the journey of championing for our children. Our approach should be peaceful whenever possible. In practical terms, this means we are called to speak to doctors, teachers, therapists, coaches, and others in our community from a position of peace rather than anger or offense. Doing so often opens doors for our children more effectively and efficiently than yelling or blaming.

I mentioned earlier that I was a teacher for several years before we started our family. In those years of teaching, I sat through countless conferences with parents, including many that focused on students with learning disabilities. I remember one particular conference for a student who was struggling with reading and writing. Everyone—the parents, classroom teachers, special education staff—was in attendance. The child's test scores were low, and the gap between her and her classmates increased daily. The need to diagnose her possible learning disabilities was crucial.

As I sat across the table from my student's parents and fellow staff members, I was the passionate teacher advocating for my student. But for all my passion, my heart was not in the right place. I was frustrated that the special education department wanted to do more evaluations and take her out of my classroom. As her classroom teacher, I felt that I knew her best, and in my pride, I felt that I could meet her academic needs. So rather than peacefully voicing my concerns, I am embarrassed to say I aggressively voiced my opinions. Rather than helping my student, I did her harm. Rather than bringing calmness to the room, I contributed to its tense atmosphere. My opinion, though valid, lost its credibility because I was combative and defensive.

I learned that day that strife and anger will not produce the results we want. Two scriptures in Proverbs serve as reminders about a better approach for problem-solving. Proverbs 15:1 says, "*A gentle answer turns away wrath, but harsh words stir up anger*" (NIV, emphasis added). Peaceful, well-thought-out words will produce better results. Harsh and angry words can stir up more trouble and move us away from successfully championing for our children.

Proverbs 15:4 says, "Gentle words *bring life and health . . .*" (TLB). It's much better to bring life and health to our children, and this comes through using words that are gentle and rooted in peace. If I want to successfully champion for my child, gentle words bring the best results. If I make a phone call, send an email, or walk into a meeting with an angry heart and harsh words, I will not see the results I desire for my daughter.

It so important that we take the time to get our hearts right before advocacy interactions—whether they are with doctors, teachers, specialists, or with members of our church or community. We need to ask God to heal us of our offenses and wounds, to ask for wisdom, and to rise up ready to take a peace-filled approach to bring the results we want and need for our children. We need to make our child the main focus, not the opposition. This focus will keep us rooted in peace and help us fight for our children instead of fighting against people or systems.

Opportunities for Advocacy

We each have daily opportunities to advocate for our children. I want to look at some of these opportunities and share a few personal experiences that have shaped the way we champion for Charlie. You may have had different experiences and a different approach to some of these opportunities, and that's okay. Every child is different, every family is different, and what works for me may not work for you, and vice versa. I am not the perfect advocate. I make mistakes, and I am still learning and growing. I can't be the perfect example, but I can point you to the Word of God that is always perfect and never changing. As we look at these levels of advocacy, I want to pull in truths and principles from the Bible. Even though we might take different approaches, we will be most effective when we advocate according to the truth and wisdom that God gives us in the Bible.

When what we do is rooted in the Word, Psalms 1:3 says that we are like a tree, healthy and growing strong, producing results and seeing progress in every season. This is a verse Luke and I pray over our Charlie—that she would be that tree "which yields its fruit in season and whose leaf does not wither," so that whatever she does prospers (Psalm 1:3, NIV).

Family First

Advocacy happens on many different levels, and it happens first with family—our spouse and our other children. Within our own family is where we first learn how to champion for our child with special needs. We advocate for them as they find their place in the family unit or, as I like to say, within the tribe. Within our tribe, we hold on to what Galatians 5:22-23 describes as the fruits of the Spirit. If we want our family to be a healthy, growing tree, like in Psalm 1:3, we must consider the fruit we are producing. We want to show love for one another, have joy, and do our best to keep a peaceful home and peace among one another. We want to have patience and be kind with our words and actions. We want to be good and do good to one another. We want to be gentle and have self-control. We want these fruits to be evident in the lives of each of our family members. These fruits are the foundation for how we want to relate to and care for Charlie, and we hope that our other children will follow our example.

Advocacy goes beyond immediate family and into extended family as well. Charlie's grandparents, aunts, uncles, and cousins—they are all watching how we interact with Charlie and how we talk about her within our family. Through these everyday interactions, we are answering these questions about her to our family:

- How should Charlie be treated?
- What will be expected of her?
- How will we make adjustments for her within the family and our daily routines?
- How should we talk about Charlie with others?
- How can we help others to know how to engage with her?

So much of what our family does and doesn't do in how we treat and talk about Charlie impacts our ability to successfully advocate for her. If we, as parents, interact with Charlie from a place of frustration (lacking the fruit of peace and patience), our other children will see that frustration and do the same. If we expect less of Charlie and do things for her—hurting her level of independence and not instilling the fruit of faithfulness—the family may follow suit. If we celebrate Charlie and invite the family to join in (the fruit of joy), they will be sure to celebrate right along with us.

March 21 is National Down Syndrome Awareness Day, a special day for families who have a loved one with Down syndrome. March is the third month of the year, and it's the twenty-first chromosome that creates the genetic uniqueness within a person who has Down syndrome. When you put these two numbers together, you get 3/21, the day we celebrate those who have three copies of the twenty-first chromosome. On this special day, we invite family and friends to celebrate with us by wearing crazy socks (joining in the Rock Your Socks campaign) and sharing posts and showing support on social media. We usually go out for ice cream, take fun pictures, and make this a special day for Charlie. We talk about Down syndrome and invite our family to celebrate the way God has made Charlie.

Celebrating 3/21 is just one of the ways we advocate for Charlie within our family. By setting aside a special day and inviting our family to participate, we are supporting and fighting for Charlie both within our family and together as a family. I encourage you to discover a similar way to celebrate your child with your family. Maybe there is a designated day or month to bring awareness to your child's diagnosis. If so, this can be a great way to champion for your child and invite your family to do the same!

At Church

Being involved in our church is one of our family's top values and priorities. My husband is in full-time ministry as a pastor. I work part-time in ministry as a worship leader and young adult ministry leader. Luke and I know we are called to build the local church and make disciples of Jesus. So much of what our family does week in and week out centers on our church schedule and activities, and I have found that our church community is another place within which I can advocate for Charlie.

The first level of advocacy, which happens in our family, extends to impact the way we champion for Charlie within our church community. When we walk through the doors of our church, we can communicate many different things about Charlie. We can communicate that she is accepted and loved within our family. We can communicate that we treat her the same as her siblings and have the same behavioral expectations. We can communicate that we want her to be included in activities created for children her age. We set the tone and the example in how to treat Charlie based on our behavior and interaction as a family.

We may also unintentionally communicate the wrong message; for example, rather than celebrating our calling to parent a child with special needs, we can let a hard day negatively impact our mood or simply miss an opportunity to champion our child. Rather than entering the church doors with a smile, a sour attitude can create a tension and awkwardness that doesn't demonstrate acceptance and love, but rather weariness and defeat. If we aren't careful with our words, we can communicate frustration, possibly enabling others to be frustrated with our child and family as well. We can communicate that we want isolation by removing ourselves and our children from ministry settings and opportunities to connect and grow in our faith.

Please understand that I'm not suggesting you put on a fake smile when you walk through the doors of your church. Church should be a place where you can be honest and feel safe. But I also want to bring attention to the impact your interactions can have on your ability to advocate for your child in *any* setting where others are watching.

Take advantage of the opportunities to make a positive impact at church. Be more than an observer; engage and own your role within the body of Christ. 1 Corinthians 12 talks about the church and how it is like a body with many parts. Every part is valuable, has something to contribute, and is necessary for the overall function of the body. "God has placed the parts in the body, every one of them, just as he wanted them to be" (1 Corinthians 12:18, NIV). Play your part and be a champion within your local church body. If systems and structures

Be more than an observer; engage and own your role within the body of Christ.

aren't in place to help support your child or other children with special needs, begin conversations and offer to help support ministry leaders to create a solution. Too many families raising a child with special needs don't find their place within the local church. They are unsure that ministry settings are prepared and appropriate to support their children, so rather than playing their part within the church, they leave and may even give up their search for a church that will provide spiritual and relationship support for their family. I believe that God wants your family to take an active role in the body of Christ, and that starts in a local church, so don't give up. God can give you the wisdom and the favor to help you find a great church that will support your child and help you grow in your faith.

We are so thankful for the love, acceptance, and support we receive for Charlie from our church family at Cornerstone. Charlie is greeted at the door and receives high fives and hellos from people passing in the hallway. She participates in her classroom activities along with her peers every week. She has been a part of camp, children's choir, and specially themed services. There are times Charlie joins us in service with the adults. She sits with us and worships right by our side. She joins us for prayer meetings. She has found her place within our church family. Adjustments have been made from time to time, and I am so thankful for the way our church has made room for Charlie and embraced our family. Unless she is physically unable to participate or isn't interested in the programs that are offered, we have always found a place for her within the church community.

If I have questions or concerns about Charlie and her interactions within our church community, I first hold them in my heart and lay them before the Lord. It helps to pray about my concerns. I also bring them to my husband, who always has a great way of helping me gain greater perspective on situations. There are even times I gather input and advice from trusted family members or close friends on the matter. Seeking counsel outside of ourselves can bring greater understanding and enable us to make the best decisions moving forward. Proverbs 11:14 says, "Where there is no counsel, the people fall; but in the multitude of counselors there is safety" (NKJV). After praying and sharing my concerns with those I love and who are spiritually minded, usually one of three things happens:

1. I realize the issue is not really something that needs to be addressed.
2. The issue resolves itself.
3. I find that I need to have a conversation with a classroom teacher or the children's minister. When this is the case, I come with gentle words from a position of peace, and I almost always see an improvement in the issue or get the insight I need to help Charlie move forward.

In Education

Education can be one of the most, if not the most, challenging areas to champion for our children. Most teachers are passionate about helping our children succeed; some, however, seem overwhelmed or disinterested in partnering with you to support your child's development. Schools can have limited resources and funding for special education resources and staffing. A school's leadership team can have varying priorities. Some schools give a lot of attention and invest financially into athletic programs, while others focus on the arts; some focus on academics, and others technology. Some give highest priority to honors and gifted programs. Not every school chooses to fine-tune their special education classrooms and staff.

I have walked through the doors of many different schools and classrooms and have interacted with several different teachers. My early experiences began in college when I was a teacher in training. I observed and taught in classrooms with high- and low-income students in the inner city and suburban communities at public and private/religious schools, early education/childcare centers, elementary campuses, middle schools, and in high school classrooms. Although my children are young, my experience has continued as we have navigated our way through various educational settings. Both Charlie and Nora (my youngest daughter) have participated in programs that support young children who are considered "at-risk" due to learning disabilities/physical impairments. All three of my children have participated in early school programming from preschool age. These many school settings, both as a teacher and a parent, have given me a lot of perspective and valuable experience that have helped me better advocate for Charlie in the classroom.

One thing I have learned about our children's school and their education is the importance of seeing their teacher as an ally. Your child's greatest advocate, outside of yourself, is their teacher. They are the ones who will be instructing, investing, and caring for your child for thirty-plus hours a week. We constantly pray that Charlie will have favor with her teachers (Luke 2:52). We pray that they will use wisdom and creativity in the classroom to help her grow academically. As we pray for our allies in the classroom, we also work to establish a positive relationship with them. This, too, is essential to successful championing.

I still remember a conversation I had with a parent years ago when I was in my first year of teaching. I was a fourth-grade teacher at a large public school in Tulsa, Oklahoma. I was meeting with the mother of one of my students after school one day to talk about his progress and behavior in the classroom. He was an excellent student who had been working hard. The mother was so thankful for his success and the growth he had recently shown in his academics. He was beginning to excel in math, and she was thrilled that he was enjoying school for the first time in his life. With tears in her eyes, she said, "I realize you are practically raising my son. You are with him more hours in the day than I am."

Her comment shocked me, and it has stuck with me to this day. I don't know if I would totally agree with the "raising her son" part, but he was in my classroom, under my care and instruction, for a majority of his day, five days a week, nine months out of the year. Apart from the parent, a teacher has one of the greatest impacts on our children and how they will develop academically, behaviorally, and socially. To engage with them as an ally is crucial.

In addition to creating a positive relationship with your child's teacher, another great way to champion for your child is to know the classroom environment they will be in each day. Most of the time, before my daughter starts in a new class, I have scheduled a time to observe her prospective classroom. During these visits, I introduce myself to the prospective teacher as Charlie's mom and begin a relationship with him or her. I ask questions, share my concerns, and work to establish open communication and a positive, professional relationship right from the start. These initial steps show my child's teacher that I am an involved parent who cares about the success of my child in their classroom.

Not only do I try to create a connection with the prospective teacher and observe the classroom setting but I also ask for suggestions and input from Charlie's current teacher. If I have established a good relationship with Charlie's current teacher, they can be a great resource in helping us champion for Charlie as she progresses from grade to grade. The current teacher knows Charlie as a student in a classroom setting. They can help evaluate whether a particular teacher and classroom we are considering might be a good fit to meet her needs. I have also found it helpful to seek out fellow parents who have had experience with the teacher we are considering for Charlie.

The truth is that not every year will be the best year in the best class with the best teacher, but as parents we can be proactive in this process and make decisions based on the information we gather. I think we can most successfully advocate for our children when we gather as much information as possible—from personal observation, other educators, and fellow parents. These resources and information, paired with prayer, help us set up our child for success in education.

And when it comes to the ongoing relationship with the teacher and school, I have found a few things to be very helpful. It's important to respond and engage in parent/teacher communication. There is something so encouraging and motivating to a teacher when they connect with a student and their family. As a teacher, when I had a relationship not only with my students but the parents as well, I felt better connected and had greater perspective. In turn, I could teach the child more effectively. The relationship motivated me as a teacher because I knew my efforts were appreciated. It made me want to work harder to help that student succeed.

Like you, I've had all sorts of experiences—both good and bad—in schools. It would be great if all I had to do was talk to the teacher and do my due diligence before I sent my child into a particular classroom, but even with all the work I do before the school year begins, bad experiences can and do happen; however, I can choose to use even the bad experiences as an opportunity to champion in a positive way. When concerns come up, I can choose to talk with the classroom teacher first. Rather than gossip with parents, I take my question or the issue to the person who can help me understand or make an adjustment as needed. Ephesians 4:29 says, "Let no corrupting talk come out of your mouths, but only such as is good for building up, as fits the occasion, that it may give grace to those who hear" (ESV). Tearing down your child's teacher with other parents isn't championing; it's a distraction from creating a solution.

I have also found that, sometimes, the cause of and solution to my concerns doesn't lie with the teacher at all but is something I can address and resolve from home. Part of effective advocacy is taking ownership of the problem. It's not always someone else's fault. There are things within my power to change at home and with my child. I have to swallow my pride and step up my game. If Charlie is still struggling with reading, it might be time for reading tutoring. If Charlie's handwriting is getting worse, we can do things from home to help her practice and make the necessary improvements. If she is being rough with her hands and not listening to her teachers, we will take ownership of those behavior problems and address them at home with the proper consequences. Let's work to be advocates who take ownership and help create solutions.

In Our Community

Another level of advocacy is within our communities. Whether I am taking Charlie to the grocery story, playing at a park, or together with family or friends at a local parade for our small town, my interaction with Charlie makes either a positive or negative impact on the way people will perceive and receive my daughter. The way I talk to her and about her, as well as the way I behave with her, has the potential to open or close hearts. If I am defensive and get easily offended by the looks people give, or the way they do or don't interact with my daughter, I am missing opportunities to show that we love Charlie, celebrate her, and that she is a blessing to our family.

As we are in our communities, we can be a light that shines brightly to show the love of God and the good work he is doing within our families (Matthew 5:16). Every time we walk out the door with our children, we can be their champions.

Beyond our physical community, there is also a virtual community we have access to as parents. Through social media, blogging, and online communities, we can champion for our children. They are powerful tools that have the potential to reach people across the world. There are people who have never met Charlie but who have read about her on my blog or seen pictures and posts about her on Facebook. I hope these people within our virtual community see a mother and

> *Every time we walk out the door with our children, we can be their champions.*

a family that is supporting and advocating for Charlie. Ultimately, I hope they see the hand of God at work in our lives so that they might be drawn to Him.

If you want to advocate in your community, begin by researching local organizations and groups that focus on what you are passionate about. If it's not out there, be the one to start it. Make it happen. Pave the way for others to join with you or follow after you. As we advocate for our children, we can connect with other parents and increase our ability to advocate and produce positive results in our community.

Sometimes negative experiences act as the catalyst for change. Rather than becoming bitter, we can choose to make things better for the families that come after us. One negative experience I had was in the hospital when we were told Charlie might have Trisomy 21. In that moment, I felt so alone, so overwhelmed, and so ill equipped to parent a child with special needs. No one gave me any resources or information about support groups in the area. They simply sent me home to figure things out on my own.

Out of that negative experience, I partnered with another parent to create "Welcome Baby" bags that included general information about Down syndrome, local support groups in the area, mentor parents they could reach out to if they had questions or needed someone to talk to, and gifts celebrating their new baby. We gave these bags to local hospitals and doctors' offices so that when a mother received the diagnosis, she could be gifted a bag as a way to provide resources and support from the beginning. We worked together to create a better experience within our community for mothers and families. It took some planning and effort on our part, but it was something simple we could do to provide the support we felt was necessary for these mothers. One young mother who received one of our "Welcome Baby" bags reached out to me, and I am still connected with her today. It has been awesome to see her thrive as a champion mom and watch her little girl grow.

There are so many creative ways to advocate within our communities. If you have an idea, go for it! Even if it encourages only one family or impacts only one child, your efforts are well worth it!

At Local and National Levels

The opportunity to advocate on larger platforms is not as common, but when God opens the door, I have two words for you: TAKE IT! Make the most of every opportunity (Ephesians 5:16) to champion for your child and share the goodness of God that is at work in your family. You may feel nervous or unqualified, but if God gives you a voice, use it. Rise up with love in your heart and peace on your lips, and be confident in what God is calling you to do and be for His glory.

I have seen God open amazing doors to advocate for Charlie. I have had the opportunity to serve as a member on the Michigan Coordinating Council for Infants and Toddlers with Developmental Disabilities (MICC). I have been honored to be a part of She Speaks for the state of Michigan, which is a group of women who are in a position of influence and leadership in various fields of business, social work, politics, and ministry across our state. People around the world have read *Chosen for Charlie: When God Gifts You with a Special-Needs Child*, my first book, and heard our testimony of what God has done and is doing in and through our daughter. I have been able to speak on the radio and television about our family and have been so honored to share our journey in raising our daughter. My mother-in-law, Charlie's grandma, had the opportunity to pray in Washington D.C. She stood on the steps of the capital building as she prayed for human life to be protected. She shared about Charlie and prayed passionately while holding up a poster of the *Chosen for Charlie* book cover. God has led our family through doors we didn't even knock on and has enabled us to champion in ways I never imagined. I am always so humbled and amazed when God creates these opportunities.

If you have a desire to advocate for your child, look for opportunities. They are out there! Start with what feels natural. If you are a writer, start a blog or write a book. If you love connecting with people, create an event that will gather and help celebrate families and children with special needs. If you love to speak or teach, ask your child's classroom teacher if you can come to their classroom or school to talk about your child. You can inspire acceptance and share how we can better understand and love those different from us. We will find many levels of advocacy available to us when we choose to rise up!

Rise up for the sake of your child's future and purpose. You will be amazed at the opportunities you have to champion and make an impact.

Great Nation, Great Glory

What impact can our advocacy have on our children? It can help them fulfill their purpose. Hagar's son had a destiny that was worth rising up for. He was the start of a great nation. God had a promise and a purpose for him. Hagar chose to rise up and fight for that promise to be fulfilled.

I don't know what God has in store for Charlie. I'm not sure what she will become or what she will pursue. Some days I ask her what she wants to do when she grows up (always a fun question to ask young children). I know that some children might respond to this question with dreams of becoming a firefighter, a professional athlete, or a ballerina. Charlie's answer to this the question isn't like what other kids her age might say. Charlie's dream for her life? She says she wants to live with her mommy and daddy—so simple and so sweet. *Yes, baby girl, there is always a place for you with Mommy and Daddy.*

I'm sure as she develops different interests, her dreams will change. As her mother, as her champion, I see great potential in Charlie. I see a passion for music. I see her love for food and cooking. I see the way she loves people, gives hugs, and interacts with those she cares about. Will music be a part of her future? Will she work in a restaurant? Will she work with people and help others? I'm not sure. But I do know that God has a plan for her and promises that her future is bright.

> "For I know the plans I have for you," declares the LORD, "plans to prosper you and not to harm you, plans to give you hope and a future."
>
> —*Jeremiah 29:11, NIV*

I love the story in John 9 where Jesus and His disciples are traveling through Jerusalem and come across a man who was born blind. The disciples look at the man and wonder why he was born that way. Jesus tells them that the man was born blind so that the "works of God might be displayed in him" (John 9:3, ESV). As we champion for our children and fight for their future, God will show Himself, His power, His love, His goodness, His faithfulness—and He will be glorified. God has plans and purposes that are at work in our children. We don't always see or understand His plans, but we can know that God will reveal Himself through it all. He has a great purpose, and His great glory will be seen.

Advocacy Impact

Moses serves as a great example of an advocate by helping us see what is possible when someone chooses to rise up. As a strong advocate for the people of Israel, his choice affected a multitude of people. God encountered Moses at the burning bush on the backside of the desert and said, "I have indeed seen the misery of my people in Egypt. I have heard them crying out . . . and I am concerned about their suffering . . . So now, go. I am sending you" (Exodus 3:7,10, NIV). Moses was chosen to be a champion who would fight for those who couldn't fight for themselves, and in His mercy and love, God called Moses to rise up and bring the children of Israel out of slavery and into the promised land.

Our call to champion can extend beyond our children to other families. God can use us to bring other families into a place of promise, peace, and purpose. Your answer to that call can impact not only your child but also other children and families within your community for years to come.

I have been powerfully impacted by mothers who have made the choice to advocate for their children. These mothers gave me courage and hope when we faced uncertain times with Charlotte. They paved the way with their advocacy and fought battles we didn't have to fight for ourselves.

I will never forget my first phone call to another mom who had a child with Down syndrome after finding out about Charlie's diagnosis. My mother has a dear friend Pam who has three children, one of whom is an adult son with Down syndrome. My mom had given me Pam's number to give her a call. I held on to her number for days before calling her. I'm not sure why I waited to dial the number; I think I was afraid of opening up to someone I had never met. I was afraid I might break down and cry and make Pam feel uncomfortable. I was even afraid I might hear a weary mother on the other side of that phone line, which would only make my heart feel heavier. I was afraid I might hear stories of her son's challenges. Maybe the conversation would be about the harsh reality and setbacks her family experienced while raising a child with Down syndrome. I was afraid of becoming more afraid.

I lay across my bed and entered her phone number into my phone. The phone began to ring. I remember looking up into my vanity mirror, giving myself that last-minute pep talk, *You can do this, you need this, talking to another mother will make you feel not so alone.* It was only a few rings before Pam picked up her end of the line, and I heard a gentle, "Hello?"

"Hi, this is Jen, Ginger's daughter. My mom gave me your phone number to reach out and call you."

"Oh, yes! Hello! I am so glad you called."

The joy and strength in Pam's voice surprised me. My fears were met with her kind and gracious words. She instantly calmed the worries I had felt only moments earlier. Our conversation flowed easily, her sharing about her son and me sharing about our Charlotte. There was a lot that was said during our thirty-minute phone call. I asked questions and shared my thoughts, feelings, fears, and pain.

There wasn't one particular thing Pam said that impacted me most, but it was the simple way she talked about her journey with her family and the wonderful impact her son had made on her faith and her perspective on life. I found the way she talked about her other children and the closeness of their family inspiring and encouraging. It was the joy, peace, and grace I heard in her voice that calmed me and filled me with hope. Pam was a champion for her son, and through that one phone call, I was inspired to become a champion for Charlie.

Another champion parent whom I continue to see rise up is the mother of one of Charlie's best friends, my dear friend Corena. As I have watched her champion for her daughter, who is a year older than Charlie, our family has been empowered to champion as well. She rallies the school to celebrate children with Down syndrome and teach the students about Down syndrome awareness. She uses her gifts as

> *It was the joy, peace, and grace I heard in her voice that calmed me and filled me with hope.*

a cosmetologist to help at the annual Tim Tebow Foundation event, Night to Shine, where she helps young men and women with special needs look and feel their best for their very own prom night. She asks the hard questions, starts conversations, and gathers resources to create the best possible opportunities—whether it's for her daughter to participate in a local dance class or leading and creating local events with AMBUCS (a national charitable organization that inspires mobility and independence) for those with special needs. She has been an incredible resource to our family and has enabled us to better champion for Charlie.

You see, as you champion for your child, other families will be empowered along the way. As you rise up, you are making a way for families to position their child to become who they are called to be. You are leading and inspiring people in ways you will never fully understand. Just as I have been encouraged by Pam, Corena, and several other champion parents, I hope to do the same as I respond to God working in my life.

There is more at stake than just our child's future. We are rising up for those who may not be able to rise up for themselves just yet. With our calling as those chosen for our children, God has promised to equip us for every championing moment that lies ahead.

Chapter 4
Chosen to Champion

You did not choose me, but I chose you and appointed you so that you might go and bear fruit—fruit that will last—and so that whatever you ask in my name the Father will give you.

John 15:16, NIV

Something I have come to believe with all my heart is that God has chosen us for our children. It is not by accident that our children were born and entrusted into our care; it is God's plan for our family and our future. A child with special needs is not a burden to bear. They are a precious gift for whom God has chosen us to fight, pray, and believe so that they might become all that God has intended them to be. We are chosen to sit on the front row of their lives, cheering them on every step of the way. We get the best view. We get to have an experience that is not for the faint of heart. We were chosen for this.

If you read my story from my first book, *Chosen for Charlie*, feel free to skim ahead. If you haven't read that book, I want to give you an inside look at our family and the journey of discovering our daughter's diagnosis and our calling to a life we never expected.

Chosen for Charlie

My husband, Luke, and I were so excited to get pregnant. We had been married almost four years. We were in our late twenties, and we felt like it was time to begin trying for our first baby. On Christmas Eve of 2011, we made a very special announcement to our family with the words "early Christmas present" written across my belly. We couldn't wait for our precious baby to arrive just nine months later.

I was thrilled to be pregnant. I experienced all the typical symptoms of pregnancy—the nausea, the fatigue, the uncomfortable nights of little sleep. But all this was worth the wait of our soon-to-arrive baby. The excitement of becoming a mother, watching Luke become a father, and caring for our first child made each month sweeter as we got closer to the due date.

Initially, all my doctors' appointments were routine, and good reports came in month after month. Then one particular ultrasound revealed something new. The measurements of baby's long leg and arm bones were coming up short. The nurse led me across the hall to talk to a specialist who sat me down to discuss the ultrasound.

In that small room, sitting across from a doctor I had never met, I heard the words I will never forget. "Do you know much about Down syndrome?" he asked. Shocked by his question, I was unable to process the words and conversation that followed. I simply sat in disbelief as he placed charts and diagrams on the table between us. The images were black and white pictures of typical strands of DNA made up of twenty-three chromosomes, each with their perfect pair. As he flipped the page, he showed me what would be different for my baby. The twenty-first chromosome looked not so perfect with its additional copy, its offset of three rather than the perfect two. That third chromosome would change everything about this baby. From the way she looked, the way she developed, the way she would behave—that tiny genetic tweak would alter her entire body and life, along with our family and our future.

I left the doctor's office stunned. I walked through the parking lot, opened the door to my car, and sat down in the driver's seat not knowing what to do next or how to process what had just happened. It was all too much to take in. Fears filled my mind, and tears began to flow as I tried to pray.

God, what just happened? My faith and thoughts battled. *Do I pray that the baby doesn't have Down syndrome? But what if she does? What if that's God's plan? Will that mean I don't want her because she isn't what I prayed for?* With all these messy questions came a bunch of messy tears for many messy months to follow.

Those months were filled with prayer, reaching out to family and friends, and believing God would give us a healthy baby girl. Baby showers came and went. More doctors' appointments continued to point to Down syndrome. Testing was offered to confirm suspicions, as was the choice to terminate my pregnancy. Without hesitation, we declined both. Testing put me and our baby girl at risk, and regardless of the diagnosis, we were keeping our baby and trusting God with the details. But growing fears and unknowns constantly challenged our desire to trust—unknowns that couldn't be answered until our baby arrived. Would Charlotte be born a healthy baby girl, or were we about to step into something we never expected for our family?

On August 10, in the middle of the night, my water broke. Luke rushed us to the hospital, where I labored for eleven hours, pushed for two, and welcomed our precious Charlotte Joy at 12:17 p.m. Looking at her tiny face, her precious blue eyes, and her tuft of strawberry blonde hair upon her head, I was so in love. Doctors initially said she was healthy, but within just a few hours, after more visits and various opinions from other doctors who examined Charlie, they decided to do a blood test to be sure.

Three days later we received a phone call. My husband answered, and the doctor wasted no time giving the difficult news. He had received the results of the blood test—positive for Trisomy 21. My body sank. My heart broke. My dreams disappeared for what I had imagined for our family and our future. For those who have a child with special needs, you know exactly what I mean when I say that part of your dreams die the day you receive the diagnosis. With that one phone call, we knew we would have to redefine our dreams for our family. We were about to go down a path we had never imagined.

After tests confirmed the diagnosis for our baby girl, I sank into a deep sadness. Nothing made sense. We had prayed and believed for a healthy child. I never imagined we would have a child with Down syndrome. I wondered if I had done something wrong. Had I not prayed hard enough? Did I lack the faith that could have healed her? I was concerned for my husband as well. I worried for him and his heartache.

I realized I knew nothing about Down syndrome and started reading and researching online. All this led to more questions and fears. All the while, God remained silent.

I had been praying day after day, "Speak, God. God, I need you. God, what is going on? How am I going to raise this child? I don't have what it takes. God I'm scared." In all these desperate prayers, I didn't hear God say anything. With little sleep and the ever-growing learning curve of being a first-time mother, I felt utterly exhausted and overwhelmed. I needed God to speak, but He wasn't, and I had come to the end of myself.

It was at the end of myself that I found a new beginning with God. I was in the shower one day and uttered a prayer that I barely had enough strength to even express: "God, if you don't speak, I'm not going to make it." And then, in that moment, in that desperate, honest, exhausted moment, God spoke.

"I chose you to be her mom."

In that simple moment, a profound work began in my heart. I was chosen. I get to be Charlie's mom. This is not a burden, but a gift to be treasured. I get to fight for her, pray for her, and champion for her.

Friend, to be chosen is to be hand-selected, to be preferred and seen as best suited. God has hand-selected us for our children. For some reason, one we may never fully know or understand, we are the ones best suited for our children.

"I chose you to be her mom."

I was chosen to be Charlie's mother. You were chosen to be the parent, grandparent, aunt, uncle, or even friend of the family who is raising a child with special needs. You get to be a part of this child's life and champion for them.

Out of the revelation that we are chosen comes a calling to champion. Even if you like the idea of being chosen, you may have some doubts about championing for your child when you look at the reality of your life. You might be thinking, *I'm not sure I have what it takes to truly be a champion for my child. I have a job. I have to take care of the house. I have to get my kids to school. I have to pay the bills. I barely have enough time and energy to make it through each day, so how can I champion for my child when feel like I am in survival mode as a parent?*

When it comes to championing for your child, you may feel like there are times when you don't have what it takes. You are tired, your resources are limited, and you are lacking hope. You feel like you don't have the strength or the vision to keep your child moving forward. There are moments of inspiration and motivation, but they might be few and far between. As time goes on and life keeps happening, it's easy to lose momentum and the energy it takes to continue pushing and fighting for the potential progress your child can make.

I want to encourage you that being chosen comes with a promise to be equipped as the champion for your child. We are going to take a look at a mother who needed God to show up and be what she couldn't for her son and her family. You may not always feel like you have what it takes to effectively champion, and that is exactly the place where God can step in to equip you in a supernatural way.

Champion Connection

If we can relate to a character in a book or a situation in a movie, it helps us to engage that much more as a reader or viewer. The same applies to the personal connections we make with the text as we read the Bible. If we can relate to the story or the person on the page, the words carry more meaning, and we can more easily find application to our own life. That's why I look for personal connections as I read God's Word. You may have heard people refer to God's Word as being alive (see Hebrews 4:12). When we connect and put ourselves into the stories we read, it can become very much alive to us.

The story I hope you'll connect with now is found in 1 Kings 17. It's a story about a mother who was caring for her child and doing the best she could to make it through each day. We don't know the details of her life or her household, but we do know that a drought had brought her to the end of herself and what she needed to keep her and her son alive. This mother was chosen for her family, and she became a champion when God supplied her with what she needed every day to rise up and care for her son.

The prophet at the time, Elijah, was in Zaraphath in the region of Sidon. There had been no rain in the land. The region was in a serious drought. God led Elijah to the town gate and instructed him to look for a widow who would give him food. He found the woman gathering sticks and asked her to get him some water and some bread. When the prophet made his request, the mother replied, "I don't have any bread—only a handful of flour in a jar and a little olive oil in a jug. I am gathering a few sticks to take home and make a meal for myself and my son, that we may eat it—and die" (1 Kings 17:12, NIV). Notice the mother's first response, "I don't have any bread." She was focused on what she didn't have.

Our Lack Brings His Provision

Sometimes we can feel like we just don't have what our children really need. Many times, I have had conversations with God that sounded like this: *God, I'm not sure I can be what Charlie needs me to be right now. I don't have the time or energy to give attention to that issue. I don't feel like I have what it takes to care for this child and give her the support she needs. I'm not enough.*

Focusing on our lack allows self-doubt and comparison to creep in. How many times have you looked at another parent who is a fierce advocate and thought to yourself, *I don't have what they have. I don't have the platform or the personality to speak up for my child and make an impact like they do.*

A choking point for our championing can be comparison. If I compare myself to others who seem to be doing more and fighting better for their child, my championing stops there. I count myself out before even considering the voice I can have for my child and what might be possible if I choose to use it. When we compare ourselves to others and focus on what we don't have, we fail to let God in to help us as parents.

It's great to gather ideas from other champion parents, but don't let comparison cause you to despise what you have. What *you* have is what *your child* needs. Remember, you are *chosen* for your child.

All too often, however, the "don't haves" are top of mind: *I don't have the resources. I don't know how to speak up about her medical needs. I don't feel qualified to reach out to other parents and encourage them. I don't have the skills to help her grow in this area.* And the sad thing is that my "don't haves" hurt not only my ego but also my child. If I allow my "don't haves" to make me feel defeated, then I kill the potential I have to champion for my child.

Don't despise your "don't haves"; rather, bring them before God in prayer. When we are honest with God about where we find ourselves, He responds and acts on our behalf. When God sees a humble heart, He gives grace (James 4:6). Our "don't haves" are an opportunity for God to step in. Our place of lack can lead us to a place of provision.

After the mother told the prophet what she didn't have, she shared what she did have: a handful of flour and a little bit of olive oil. It wasn't much to her, but even in her lack, she didn't hold back what she could offer. She wasn't stingy or selfish; she shared with the prophet what she was able to give.

You may not feel like you have much to give, but God isn't asking for anything more than what you already have. As this story unfolds, we will see what God does when this mother chooses to surrender and give what she has in response to the prophet's request. Before God does something miraculous, though, the prophet prepares her heart to be full of faith and not fear.

Don't Be Afraid

If you feel overwhelmed or hopeless about the future, be encouraged that you are perfectly positioned for opportunity. You are set up for provision and breakthrough. When you are at the end of yourself, you have an advantage: You have an opportunity to move into a miracle for you and your child.

The woman in this story found a miracle in the form of a request that defied reason:

Elijah said to her, "Don't be afraid. Go home and do as you have said. But first make a small loaf of bread for me from what you have and bring it to me, and then make something for yourself and your son."

—1 Kings 17:13, NIV

Don't be afraid. *Eh-hem* (clearing my throat). *Excuse me? "Don't be afraid?" Do you know who you're talking to, Elijah?* Elijah must not have realized he was talking to a mother. Mothers have mastered many things—the art of multitasking, functioning on minimal sleep, making a gourmet meal out of a sparse pantry and an empty fridge—and, most of all, we have mastered fear.

We know how to imagine the worst for our children. As I watch my kids climb the ladder on the playground, my fear causes me to see one wrong step leading to a broken neck. As I check on my children one more time before I sneak off to bed, my fear causes me to think they have stopped breathing, and I quickly put my hand in front of their mouth to be sure I can feel their breath. As I send my kids off to school on a cool, fall morning, my fear sends them out the door in all their winter gear because hypothermia might set in during the twenty-foot walk to their dad's car. Mommas know one thing very well, and that is how to be afraid.

"Don't be afraid." As we try to connect with this mother and apply her story to raising our child with special needs, we have to recognize the fears we have for our children.

Be honest with yourself as you consider what you fear for your child. Do you fear for their academic success and failures? Do you have fears about their friendships or ability to connect with peers? Do you fear the next doctor's appointment on the calendar? Do you fear the future? Do you worry about your child's ability to become independent? Do you fear they might never get married or have a family of their own?

When we stop to admit our fears out loud, we may notice that, while some are based in the present, many are things we forecast for our future.

> *Therefore do not worry about tomorrow, for tomorrow will worry about itself. Each day has enough trouble of its own.*
> —Matthew 6:34, NIV

The Bible warns us to focus on today and not worry about tomorrow. Worrying about the future only steals joy from today. If we spend all our time worrying about the what-ifs down the road, we will miss the beautiful pit stops with our children right here and right now. Choosing peace and trust over fear and worry is a discipline that takes effort on a daily basis. Our love for our children drives us to do all we can to care for them, but if we let go of control and let God care for our family, trusting Him for the daily needs of our children, we can begin to take hold of a life rooted in peace.

Give What You Have

After Elijah tells the mother not to be afraid, he asks her to do something *in that moment* that could have an impact on her and her family *for that day*. But Elijah tells her that if she would give him what she had in that moment, God would do something for her in return:

> *For this is what the LORD, the God of Israel, says: "The jar of flour will not be used up and the jug of oil will not run dry until the day the LORD sends rain on the land." She went away and did as Elijah had told her.*
> —1 Kings 17:14–15, NIV

If she would give to the man of God what she had, there would be provision for her and her son each and every day. They would have enough. I know we are in a different situation than this mother; after all, God probably isn't going to ask us to give up our oil and flour. But if we look at our lives, we each have something we can give to God right now. It may not seem like much, but if we give what we have with a heart that seeks to honor God and see His power at work in our lives and in the lives of children, I think we will be amazed to see God work where our resources end and His provision begins.

What do we have that we can give God? Time—we can give God our time. Time is one of the most precious things we have. Time is something we feel like we never have enough of. Giving God our time is such a beautiful sacrifice that honors Him. We can start our day with a prayer and open our Bibles to read and study His Word, which may require organizing our morning a little better to create that time for Him. Rather than scrolling through our phone, we can set it down and talk to God about our family and our needs for that day.

And that's what God wants. He wants our hearts. God wants our attention. He wants a relationship with you and with me. God is not looking for good works; He's looking for a genuine heart that is open and is inviting Him into the most precious parts of our lives. He knows our needs and the needs of our children before we even speak them (Matthew 6:8). What He is looking for is a heart that wants to know Him (2 Chronicles 16:9).

> *He's looking for a genuine heart that is open and is inviting Him into the most precious parts of our lives.*

When I prioritize God and my relationship with Him, I have found that the other parts of my life fall into place. When I spend time with God and give Him what I have, He has a way of sorting out the details of my life (Matthew 6:33). He gives me wisdom. He gives me peace. He gives me strength. He gives me grace. He takes care of the daily needs of my children and our family, just like He did for the mother and her son in our story. If we want to champion successfully for our children, we have to keep God first.

As we give God our time, seek Him in prayer, and devote ourselves to knowing Him through His Word, He will give us what we need to live this life and care for our children. He will give us strength to parent. He will give us wisdom to make decisions. He will give us favor with teachers. He will give us creative solutions to solve problems. And He does this not because we do good works or exhaust our efforts but because we give Him ourselves. My motivation for seeking God is not what He can do for me, but it's an amazing part of who He is. God is faithful to meet our needs. Matthew 6:33 says, "But seek first the kingdom of God and his righteousness, and all these things will be added to you" (ESV). God is so good to meet our needs as we give Him the simple things that we have—our time and our hearts.

He's Got You, Momma

God will take care of both you and your child as you put Him first, just as He did for the widow and her son.

> *So there was food every day for Elijah and for the woman and her family. For the jar of flour was not used up and the jug of oil did not run dry, in keeping with the word of the LORD spoken by Elijah.*
>
> *—1 Kings 17:15–16*

Both the mother *and* the son had what they needed for each day when the mother was obedient to do what Elijah asked of her.

It is easy to become so consumed with the needs of our children that we neglect our own needs. There are days I make sure my kids brush their teeth before heading out the door, but as I walk out the door behind them, I pause and wonder, *Did I brush my teeth?* I make sure my kids have clean clothes to wear each day, but I can survive in a hoodie and pair of yoga pants for a few days before I need to do a wash. I make sure they are eating balanced meals and healthy snacks and drinking enough water, but here I am eating when (or *if*) I remember and pouring another cup of coffee instead of making myself stop to eat a proper meal.

Beyond our physical needs, we also have emotional, mental, and relational needs. Friend, God cares about all the needs you have and wants to care for those needs. He made you, designed you, and knows exactly what you need to function and thrive as a parent, a spouse, in your workspace, and within your community. And He cares about meeting those needs. Trust God to care not only for your child but for you as well. He's got you, Momma. Open your heart to Him. Talk to Him and give Him what you are carrying, whatever it is that is weighing you down. Like the widow, be honest about your needs, and with a willing heart, give God what you have. As you do these things, God will meet your needs as well as the needs of your child.

Equipped for the Calling

God asks us to give Him what we have—our heart and our time. He knows what we lack, and He generously provides for our needs.

As you experience this truth in your life, it won't be long before you find yourself ready to give of yourself to meet others' needs. As God equips you to champion, you will find His provision allows you to impact and encourage others as well. This looks different for every parent champion. Some might have time to take another parent out for coffee who is earlier in their journey and needs some encouragement with raising their child. Some parents might have ideas for helping their child's school take one step closer to inclusion and creating opportunities to celebrate and encourage acceptance among their peers. Some might have a voice in their church and want to create a small group for mothers who need time and fellowship with other mothers who can relate to the challenges they are facing with their children. God might ask you to give different things in different seasons. I encourage you to be obedient and watch what God can do as you continue to step into your calling of being chosen to champion for your child!

In the next chapter, we will explore the most effective way we can champion for our children. The greatest equipping comes when we choose to do something that is both practical and powerful. Our championing goes to the next level when we choose to be parents who pray.

Chapter 5
Pray to Win

But thanks be to God! He gives us the victory through our Lord Jesus Christ.

—1 Corinthians 15:57, NIV

You've probably heard the expression "play to win." Playing to win means playing with a competitive edge and with your head in the game. It means playing not just to have fun, but with the intent of coming out on top.

When I was younger, I made almost everything a competition with my friends—from grades to goals scored in a soccer game, and even who was the tallest. If something could have a competitive twist to it, I took on the challenge. As I got older, my competitive nature seemed to cause unwanted tension in relationships. I also realized that there were more and more things that I wasn't the best at. I chose to soften my competitive edge. Rather than playing to win, I chose just to play.

I still have a competitive spirit when it comes to the things I care about most. I'm speaking, of course, about a game played on an entirely different field, where what is at stake is not my pride, but something or someone I love. When it comes to that which is most important to me—the people I love and God's purpose for my life—it's worth fighting for. I am all in. My competitive edge remains sharper than ever for my family, my friends, our local church, and God's plans for my life.

I may not play to win the same kind of competitions I did when I was younger, but now, more than ever, I play to win because the stakes are much higher. And friend, I have had to up my game. It goes beyond playing to win. It takes something much more strategic and powerful. The advantage, the secret weapon, the winning play is found in the decision to pray. Friend, let's be parents who choose to *pray to win.*

I want to win battles for my children. I want to win battles for my marriage. I want to win battles over stress, anxiety, and fear. I want to win battles over depression. I want to win physical battles and mental battles that come my way more and more.

I am sure you would say the same. The battles just keep on coming, and you don't have to lose. In fact, when you have put your faith in Christ, you can stand on the promise delivered in 1 John 5:4, that "everyone born of God overcomes the world. This is the victory that has overcome the world, even our faith" (NIV). The longer we live, the more frequent the battles and the stronger the opponent can get. Let's choose to have a competitive edge over the opposition and pray to win as we champion for our children.

Essential Ingredient

It would be impossible to talk about parenting and championing for our children without talking about prayer. Prayer is the essential ingredient that makes all the difference.

If you have ever baked, you know there are ingredients you can't do without. Growing up, my mom made lots of yummy treats in the kitchen—delicious monkey bread, hot, fresh donuts, her famous Garfield Cat cake (it wasn't about the cake, but the shape of the cake pan she used). But the most famous of all was her peanut butter Rice Krispies treats. My mouth waters even now as I think about them. This dessert disappeared faster than any other in our house. As it sat on the white tile counter of our kitchen in a glass baking dish, our family would consume an entire batch in a matter of just a few days. Being the super awesome mom that she is, she even let us believe it was a good breakfast option. She drew our attention to the main ingredients: rice cereal and peanut butter. Great options for breakfast, right? *Hmmm.* I will let you make your own decision about that. As a mother of three who bakes treats for her family, I now know the recipe goes way beyond these two ingredients. It also has sugar, lots of sugar. Really not the best breakfast option, but the tradition must continue, so yes, my kids eat them for breakfast too.

I can't even count the number of times I have made her peanut butter Rice Krispies treats. Although there are only a few simple ingredients, there is one that truly makes a difference. This is an ingredient that must not only be included but must be added in the right quantity so that the quality of the final product is ensured. Too much or not enough totally alters the taste. This essential ingredient is in the name of the treat itself and makes them simply irresistible—peanut butter. You need a full jar of peanut butter, ready to generously scoop and melt over the heated sugar. (I hope I didn't lose you to the kitchen, but if I did, go grab a treat and then come back to keep reading. I don't want you to miss this next part.)

Prayer is our essential ingredient to parenting and our ability to effectively champion for our children. The longer I live, the longer I parent, the more I realize that prayer is not and cannot be seen as something I do just when it's convenient. I can't just scrape the jar; I need a generous helping of prayer to melt through, cover, and overflow into all the pieces of my life.

You may agree that, yes, prayer is great, but it may not be something you always think about or even feel very confident doing. Maybe you feel like prayer is mysterious, intimidating, or uncomfortable, or maybe you aren't quite sure where to start.

We all have our different experiences when it comes to prayer. Maybe you had a grandma who prayed faithfully for you, and you are so thankful for her commitment to pray you through challenging times of your life. Maybe prayer is something you just did at the dinner table with your family growing up. Maybe you have memories of prayer at your church—prayers that sounded good coming from the pastor or leader on stage, but that you could never imagine saying on your own.

Maybe you pray regularly. You take time each day to pray for your family, you ask God to bless your day, you even offer to pray for others when you know they are hurting or sick. Or perhaps you are someone who thinks about praying, but you worry about doing it wrong. Maybe you think you've got to get your life straightened out before God even wants you praying to Him.

Champion for Charlie

Whatever your thoughts are on prayer, I want you to know this: Prayer is not meant to push us away from God but to pull us in close to Him. It can seem like a mystery, but prayer is simply a conversation with God. To pray is to talk to God. It is as simple as sharing about anything and everything. It is a connection point between you and your Creator.

There are times I connect with God when no one is around. There are times I connect with God when I am surrounded by people. I pray when I'm happy. I pray when I'm angry. I pray short prayers, and I pray long prayers. I pray when I feel like it and when I don't feel like it. I pray in the morning, I pray in the afternoon, and I pray at night. Hebrews 4:16 tells us that we can approach God with confidence and that His mercy and grace will be there to help us in our time of need. We can pray anytime, anywhere.

What about you? When do you pray? Where are you most comfortable talking to God? If you aren't much of a praying parent, let me encourage you to start somewhere. Maybe it's in the car after you drop your kids off at school or on your way to work. Maybe it's when you lay your head down on your pillow at night or when you walk your dog. Don't overcomplicate it. Just start somewhere because as you do, I believe God will meet you in those times of prayer.

Friend, to pray for our children is to champion for them. Prayer is an essential strategy and the most powerful advantage we have when it comes to supporting our children and helping them become who God intends them to be.

I often look at Charlie and just wonder. I wonder what she is thinking. I wonder what she understands. I wonder what she thinks about when she lays her head down at night. I wonder how she feels about her family, her friends, her daily routine. I wonder if her behavior is intentional or a result of not fully understanding expectations and norms in a given environment. There is a lot about Charlie I don't understand. But I know and am thankful for the access I have to the One who made her, knit her together (Psalm 139:13), counts the hairs on her head (Luke 12:7), and hears every thought in her mind. When I pray for Charlie, I can talk to the One knows her best and ask Him for the wisdom I need to parent her. She may be a mystery to me, but to her Maker, she is an open book. And as I go to God in prayer for her, He just might let me take a peek at some of those pages.

History Made

If we can discover the effects of prayer and the impact it can have, I believe we will be inspired to champion for our children through prayer. There are significant historical figures who recognized the impact prayer made on their lives. Here are a few powerful stories that can encourage us as we pray for our children. Take a look at these faith heroes in history who made a great impact as a result of mothers who championed for them through prayer. The following excerpts come from an article by Sharon Glasgow called "Mothers: Changing History through Prayer."

> John Wesley, one of the greatest evangelists of the 1700s (speaking to crowds of twenty thousand people or more), was raised by a mother who prayed. Susannah Wesley raised John in a home dedicated to the Word of God and prayer. In the midst of raising ten children, she would spend two hours a day in prayer herself. Many days she couldn't find a place of solitude, so she would lift her apron over her head to be alone with God. There she would pray among the children playing about her. Often her husband was gone for long lengths of time, leaving her as a single parent. Another of her other children, Charles Wesley, wrote over 9,000 hymns that we still sing today.

~

> George Washington, the father of our country, changed the course of American history for God's glory. His overwhelming reputation of humility, perseverance, dignity, honor, strength, and sincerity was second to none. He was not just a military and revolutionary hero; he was a shining example of one enlisted in the army of God. The King of kings was his leader and none other. George's mother, Mary Washington, raised him and his siblings as a single mother after his dad

died when he was ten. She found her strength in God alone. It is recorded that she went to a nearby rock outside of her house to pray continually. George wrote letters to his mother while on the battlefield of the Revolutionary War proving what her prayers were doing for him. He wrote that he escaped death when bullets went through his coat and his horses were shot out from under him. Miracle after miracle happened to George, and he honored his mother with these words: "All that I am I owe to my mother." George Washington knew many of his triumphs happened because of his mother's pleading prayers on his behalf. She prayed diligently and birthed our nation a God-fearing courageous leader.

Billy Graham, the Moses of our day, led nearly 3 million people out of spiritual bondage into freedom in Christ and preached the gospel to more than 80 million people in his lifetime. He said that of all the people he had ever known, his mother had the greatest influence on his life. She would gather the family to listen to the Bible and have prayer together in the presence of God. She and his dad would pray for Billy every morning at 10 o'clock.

Oh, if we will champion for our children through prayer, the possibilities are endless. If we would choose to pray for our children like Susanna Wesley, Mary Washington, or Morrow Graham, we could join this league of praying champions. More than simple prayers that our children would have a good day, do well on a spelling test, or make a goal during the soccer game, we can pray that God would use our children to be history makers and world changers. We can pray that God would show His glory and power in and through them so that they might make an impact for generations to come.

Offense and Defense

Prayer is not a passive act. Some people may view prayer as something simple, quiet, unintrusive. But I believe it is just the opposite. When offered up to the Lord who goes before us (Deuteronomy 31:8), fights for our children (Exodus 14:14), is all-powerful (Psalm 147:5), all-present (Psalm 139:7–12), and all-knowing (1 John 3:20), and who is limitless and able to do the impossible (Luke 1:37), prayer is powerful. When I can lay my concerns and petitions before God, the King of kings and Creator of heaven and earth, I have more than a fighting chance for my child. My child can walk into miracles and overcome in every way. Through prayer, my child can overcome what doctors predict, teachers foresee, and society expects—through prayer I have the greatest offense and defense.

In the Old Testament, the people of Judah were called by Nehemiah to rebuild the walls of Jerusalem. The city and the wall were a heap of rubble after their enemy had destroyed Jerusalem years earlier. Now it was time to restart, rebuild, and move forward. As Nehemiah gathered the people of God to begin rebuilding the walls, there was something they needed to do to ensure protection and proper security so that what was built would not be threatened by enemies or outside intruders.

> *From that day on, half of my men did the work, while the other half were equipped with spears, shields, bows and armor. The officers posted themselves behind all the people of Judah who were building the wall. Those who carried materials did their work with one hand and held a weapon in the other, and each of the builders wore his sword at his side as he worked.*
>
> —*Nehemiah 4:16–18, NIV*

While they were building the wall, there was something expected of them that would ensure the safety of their work: they had to simultaneously build and protect. They built the wall with one hand and held a sword in the other. They were on the offense and defense while doing the work.

This is a great picture for us as we pray and champion for our children. When we pray for our children, we are both building and protecting the work of God in their life. Prayer is the greatest offense and defense for our children. Prayer protects, guards, and deflects the enemy and his attempts to come against that which God is building through His people.

My friend, your child's life is being built by the Lord. Let me encourage you to stand guard and protect that work with a sword (God's Word) in your hand and prayer on your lips.

Passing the Baton

Not long ago, I was talking with a friend who also has a daughter with Down syndrome. We stood in her kitchen having mom talk as our girls played outside. We shared recent stories of funny moments we have had with our girls—the things they say, their cute mannerisms. Soon the conversation shifted toward the unknowns of our girls' future adolescent years. We began sharing with each other some of the things we worry our daughters will encounter as they get older: challenges among peers and friendships, self-care and awareness, and how they will relate to the opposite sex.

As we were discussing some of our worries, I remembered the many things from which my parents guarded and protected me while I was growing up. My parents' prayers were going before me as a shield. I believe that their prayers surrounded my life from a very early age.

My mother and father are truly heroes in the faith. Their love for God and desire to be faithful and obedient to His plan for their life and our family have made a profound impact on my life. They have lived out a humble, steadfast faith that is rooted in the Word of God and prayer. These prayers had and continue to have incredible power and influence in my life. There were the prayers they said with us as children as they tucked us into bed each night. There were the family prayers at the dinner table spoken over warm chicken and rice casserole. But even as a child, I knew their prayers went deeper and stretched further than my bedside and the dinner table.

When I look back and consider all the times God protected me from situations that should have led me down a road to sin or pain,

I know their prayers were at work. In the dark times in my life when I've felt overcome by anxiety, their prayers pulled me out by the grace of God and set me free. In the times when I was in the wrong places at the wrong time and God sovereignly protected me from harm, or the times my health failed and a doctor's diagnosis cast a shadow on my future, the prayers of my parents ushered in my safekeeping and healing.

You might be able to look back at your life and recall the same types of situations. You can remember the mother or father, the grandparent or friend, the pastor or mentor who prayed you through, prayed you out, prayed you to the other side of your valley. And if you didn't have a foundation of prayer laid for your life, you can make the change for the next generation. You can choose to be the parent who prays for their children.

I am so thankful for the prayers of my parents. Rather than worrying about Charlie and the unknown future, I remind myself of what has been passed on to me, my parents' commitment to praying for those they love. Through prayer, I can champion for my children the way my parents have championed for me. Let's choose to rise up and take hold of the power prayer can bring as we champion for our children.

Strike the Ground

Let's make a connection to another story in the Bible. This story encourages us to champion for our children through prayer in a way that is full of passion and strength. If we want God to truly intervene and work in power on behalf of our children, we have to go beyond simple prayers of blessing and daily requests.

In 2 Kings 13, Jehoash, the king of Israel in Samaria, turned to the prophet Elisha for help. Jehoash's enemies, the Arameans, were headed his way, and the king was desperate for rescue. As Jehoash watched the enemy approaching his kingdom, he hurried to Elisha, and even though Elisha was ill, he responded to the desperate king's plea and gave what might seem like an unusual set of instructions.

Elisha instructed King Jehoash to do two simple things. First, he told the king to get a bow and some arrows and shoot out the east window (1 Kings 13:15–17). This would signify a coming victory that the king would destroy the Arameans who were closing in on them. Then, as a second act of obedience and faith, Elisha told the king to strike the ground with the arrows.

> *Then he said, "Take the arrows," and the king took them. Elisha told him, "Strike the ground." He struck it three times and stopped. The man of God was angry with him and said, "You should have struck the ground five or six times; then you would have defeated Aram and completely destroyed it. But now you will defeat it only three times."*
>
> —2 Kings 13:18–19, NIV

The simple act of striking the ground represented something very significant. It was an act of faith and obedience that ultimately pointed to the potential victory and success of King Jehoash and his army. He only struck the ground three times, so he would only defeat his enemy three times. King Jehoash should have hit the ground many more times. His half-hearted efforts would yield a half-hearted reward.

So how does Jehoash's story connect to us as we champion for our children in prayer? Striking the ground can represent our act of prayer.

Every time I pray for Charlie, I am striking the ground for her. When I pray for her thyroid to function properly, I am striking the ground. When I pray for her ability to communicate and understand language, I am striking the ground. When I pray for her protection from people and situations that might bring her harm, I am striking the ground. The more I pray, the more I strike the ground, and the more I strike the ground, I believe the more ground is taken for her victory and the more God's divine hand and protection covers her life. Praying is my act of faith in response to the calling I have as a parent.

Every time you pray for your child, you are striking the ground to bring victory in their life. God sees and hears every prayer you "strike." Know that each strike is a demonstration of your faith and trust in Him and His power to bring the victory. When you strike, He listens. When you believe, He will respond.

I love this word *strike* for us as praying parents. When we strike the ground, we are praying with precision, passion, and focus. We choose to get specific about our requests for our children. We move from general prayers to specific needs and issues. We get passionate in the way we pray, making prayer a priority rather than just something we remember to do sporadically. We get focused as we strike, even if we have to do it several times over, because we know that every time we pray that prayer, even if it's the same one we repeat over and over for weeks, months, even years, it will be worth it. Victory will come for our children. We choose to believe that as we champion for our children through prayer, God will respond.

An Exchange

I want to take this act of prayer one step further. When it comes to our children, we may be momma bear or papa bear, but in all reality, we do not always know what is best for our children. We are not able to see situations and circumstances beyond the present and our personal perspective. We can speculate and analyze, but we are limited in our ability to know what is absolutely best for them. Thankfully, we have access to the One who does. The God of heaven formed and created our children. He knows all, sees all, and can do all. So we can bring our championing requests to God. We can pray for the doctors' visits, the academic progress, the emotional and social needs. We can pray for protection and favor. We can pray for wisdom in how to discipline and create routines that will help our children thrive and develop independence. We can pray for the best teachers, best doctors, and best results. We can pray for great friendships. We can pray for their faith and understanding of God's love for them. Our list can go on and on. And as we pray, we hand this list over to God.

The God of heaven formed and created our children. He knows all, sees all, and can do all.

Our prayer can move beyond a list and step into an exchange. We don't just give God a list of prayers; ultimately, we give Him our children and ourselves. Only God has the wisdom to know the whats and whens that are best for our children and for His glory.

When Christ prayed in the garden before He went to the cross, He laid His request before God that the cup would pass from Him. He didn't want to suffer and endure the cross, but He chose to exchange His desire for God's greater purpose. He laid down his will and stepped into the will of His Father (Luke 22:42).

As we pray and advocate for our children, we can go beyond our list of requests and concerns and align ourselves with what God ultimately wants for our children. We can pray like Jesus, "Not my will but yours be done. God, I want all these things for my child, but ultimately, I pray Your will and Your ways above my own. I trust in Your wisdom because You are good. You know what is best for my child, for our family, and You are doing a greater work that I want to surrender to and step into."

This exchange is not an easy one. There have been times when I wanted God to do things differently, times I didn't understand why He would allow something to happen to Charlie—another trip to the emergency room or steps that seemed to move her backward instead of forward. I can spend my life wrestling with God and questioning the things He allows to happen, or I can walk in the kind of peace Isaiah 26:3 talks about: "You will keep in perfect peace those whose minds are steadfast, because they trust in you" (NIV). Lord knows a mother's heart could use more peace! We can all have that peace when we choose to give God our list of prayer requests and begin fully trusting His will and purposes for our families.

My Personal Prayers

To close this chapter, I want to share a few personal prayers I say for Charlie, Owen, and Nora. As you read these prayers, you might want to use them to pray for your children as well.

> From Luke 2:52 (NIV): *"And Jesus grew in wisdom and stature, and in favor with God and man."*

Lord, I pray that Charlie would continue to grow in wisdom and in stature and in favor with God and man. God, help her mind and body to strengthen and develop more and more every day. May she not be stunted or lacking in any area. I pray that we would see growth in her ability to read, write, and understand concepts. I pray she would have favor with doctors, teachers, her peers, people at church, and people in the community. And Lord, I pray that she would have favor with You, that You would go before her, fight for her, protect her, and keep Your eye on her everywhere she goes. I pray that You would guard her heart and life from wickedness in this world and cause her to be a shining light as Your favor rests on her.

From Psalm 1:3 (NIV): *"That person is like a tree planted by streams of water, which yields its fruit in season and whose leaf does not wither—whatever they do prospers."*

Lord, I pray that Charlie would be like that tree, planted by rivers of water, bearing fruit in every season, not withering but prospering. God, let Charlie be planted in You. I pray she would give her heart and life to You at a young age. I pray that she would find Your love. May she be planted in You and who You say she is. I pray she would bear the fruit of the spirit—love, joy, peace—that she would be patient with her brother and sister, and that she would be kind with her words and hands. I pray that she would be good and do good, even when no one is looking. I pray she would be faithful, that she could finish what she starts, complete tasks and keep commitments—staying mentally engaged, physically able, and that she would be gentle and self-controlled. God, give us wisdom to help her use her words with gentleness, to not get angry easily, but to be loving and kind. Lord, I pray her body, her mind, and her heart would never wither, but that she would prosper in every season. May she prosper spiritually, socially, physically, and mentally.

From Psalm 84:7 (NIV): *"They go from strength to strength..."* and 2 Corinthians 3:18 (NIV) *"... We are being transformed into his image with ever-increasing glory..."*

> Lord, I pray that Charlie would go from strength to strength and glory to glory. Lord, would her body and mind get stronger and stronger each day. I pray that as she grows in strength and overcomes physical, mental, and emotional challenges, Your glory would be revealed more and more. I pray that as people see Charlie, they would see Your glory. Help us to give You glory, testify of what You are doing, and use Charlie's life to show Your strength and power and how amazing You are!

Let's pray to win! Let's not forget or neglect this essential ingredient to effectively champion for our children. Let's watch our kids make history as a result of our prayers. Let's use prayer to simultaneously be on the offense and defense for our children. The baton of prayer is in our hands—let's strike the ground, again and again. And in our times of prayer, may there be a beautiful exchange of our will and desires for the will and desires that God has for us and our children.

As we become champions for our children, we can add something to the way we advocate, something that takes grit and goes hand in hand with the way that we pray. We need to pair our prayers with the grit of gratitude.

Chapter 6
The Grit of Gratitude

Give thanks in all circumstances.

—*1 Thessalonians 5:18, NIV*

With three young children, countless lessons happen in our home each day—lessons teaching the value of being responsible, showing kindness, sharing with others, and forgiveness. It is a daily effort to instill values and character in our children. One of the values we want our children to develop is gratitude.

As we help our children develop into kind and caring people, we remind them often to use three simple words: "Say thank you." Whether it's in response to refilling their juice, getting them a snack, or helping them put on their shoes, we remind our children time and time again to say thank you.

As adults, the discipline of showing gratitude is just as important. We can show gratitude in our families, among our friends, and in our workplaces. Our gratitude also extends to our faith and the way we respond to God. In the previous chapter, we looked at prayer, its importance, and its impact. In order to pray as champion parents, we must remember the encouragement in 1 Thessalonians 5:17–18 to "pray without ceasing, in everything giving thanks . . ." (NKJV).

Giving thanks. In everything. Let us be intentional about recognizing God's goodness as He works in our lives by expressing our gratitude.

We can show our gratitude through the words we pray and the attitude we have as we champion. Taking time to acknowledge how God is moving, recognizing His faithfulness, and expressing our thankfulness requires a special type of courage and determination in the face of constant opposition and challenge. Yes, gratitude takes grit. When the norm is to worry and focus on the challenges we are facing with our children, we can choose to be thankful, express gratitude, and have an overcoming attitude that celebrates what God is doing. To live grateful is to live differently, and it's an attitude that sets our championing apart.

I love when my children are grateful. As parents, our children's gratitude makes us want to bless them even more. And I believe the same is true with God. He loves it when His children, you and I, have a grateful heart. He loves to bless and move in the lives of those who are thankful and have the grit of gratitude.

Bigger Picture

As we champion for our children, we can easily become focused on the negative and the areas that need attention. We tune in to the details of what is wrong and focus on what we need to do to make it better. This is both the strength and weakness of a championing parent—while fighting for what is possible in the future, we can lose sight of the positives in the present. We busy ourselves with planning for the next evaluation or setting up the next therapy. We might even complain about the hard day we had or the frustration we are feeling with our child. We become so tuned in to the challenges of raising a child with special needs that we fail to give attention to the good that God is doing.

Taking a step back and looking at the bigger picture—not just what is happening in the moment, but all that has happened in our children's and families' lives—reminds us of God's sustaining provision for our families. From this wider angle, we can see how He blesses us with daily grace and wisdom to parent and care for our children. With the full picture in view, we can see the simple, sweet moments of blessing and joy that God allows us to share with our children. Rather than getting caught up in what needs to be fixed, we can recognize that God is protecting our children and providing for them.

If I spent all my time and energy being consumed with the areas in which Charlie needs to grow, I would miss out on the precious moments of being her mom. By pausing and appreciating the small things, like when Charlie crawls into our bed each morning and cuddles under the covers with us, I can be thankful that we have a daughter who is affectionate and loves her mommy and daddy. When she invites me to her room to play kitchen and cook food with her, I can see that

> *Champion parents live with their eyes on the bigger picture.*

she loves to imagine and might want to work in a restaurant someday. When she wants me to dance to GoNoodle with her and play tag, I can be thankful that we have a way to connect. When I see Charlie get on the bus each day, I can be thankful that she has a school that she loves. I must continue to pray about Charlie's needs and the concerns we have for her, but I must also pay attention to and be grateful for these sweet moments when I can see who she is and what God is doing in her.

What about you? What can you be thankful for as you consider the bigger picture of your child's life? Champion parents live with their eyes on the bigger picture, simultaneously looking beyond the moment while praying for present concerns. They have the grit of gratitude. They can see evidence of God's faithfulness and work in their lives and be grateful for what He has done and what He is doing. But it takes work to develop this kind of grateful grit. It takes discipline.

Developed Discipline

When I was a young girl, my youth pastor challenged me to grow in the area of gratitude by making a daily list of five things I was grateful for. Simple enough, right? But the twist was that I could never repeat something twice. I had to list different things every day.

Day One was a breeze.
1. Thank you for my family.
2. Thank you for my friends.
3. Thank you for my house.
4. Thank you for my health.
5. Thank you for my dog.

Each day, the challenge to be thankful for something different, never repeating the same thing twice, became more and more difficult. By the time I got to day twenty, the things I was thankful for took much more thought.
1. Thank you for forgiving me for the way I talked to my sister.
2. Thank you for helping me understand my chemistry assignment today.
3. Thank you that my family could sit around the table tonight for dinner.
4. Thank you for giving me the courage to invite my friend to church.
5. Thank you that my mom and dad love each other.

What started as a simple challenge from my youth pastor became a life lesson. I learned how to look closely for the good work of God in my life, and in doing so, I was developing the grit of gratitude.

When we choose to look for the good in our lives and the lives of our children, our outlook on life changes. In a world where it is normal to complain about our circumstances, we can live differently if we discipline ourselves to celebrate and be grateful.

The Grateful Leper

Let's take a look at the book of Luke, where the grit of gratitude made all the difference for a man who had an encounter with Jesus. Luke tells us there were ten men in a certain village who had leprosy, a painful skin disease that was common at the time. They were outcasts whom society considered unclean. Their disease affected their bodies, their relationships, and their future, leaving them feeling rejected and in despair. They had no hope, at least not until Jesus crossed their path one day on his way to Jerusalem.

Now on his way to Jerusalem, Jesus traveled along the border between Samaria and Galilee. As he was going into a village, ten men who had leprosy met him. They stood at a distance and called out in a loud voice, "Jesus, Master, have pity on us!" When he saw them, he said, "Go, show yourselves to the priests." And as they went, they were cleansed.

—Luke 17:11–14, NIV

Jesus miraculously healed ten lepers in an instant! The pain of their disease, the rejection they had experienced, the hopeless future that was there just moments before—all of it was erased and replaced when Jesus miraculously healed them. What an incredible day it was for these ten men! They could be restored to their families, be welcomed back into society, and live a normal existence. I imagine they were filled with joy and a renewed passion for life. In all their excitement, these ten men all had the same opportunity to show gratitude, but only one healed leper showed grateful grit.

One of them, when he saw he was healed, came back, praising God in a loud voice. He threw himself at Jesus' feet and thanked him—and he was a Samaritan. Jesus asked, "Were not all ten cleansed? Where are the other nine? Has no one returned to give praise to God except this foreigner?"

—Luke 17:15–18, NIV

Just one man had the courage to return and thank his Healer. He praised God and threw himself at Jesus' feet in gratitude. His grit of gratitude caused him to drop to his knees and give honor and glory to the One who heard his cry and healed his body.

When was the last time you showed this kind of gratitude? How often do you stop to tell God thank you for meeting a need or answering a prayer you had for your child? As champion parents, our prayers are constant. How constant is your gratitude in response to those answered prayers? Don't miss the opportunity to show gratitude because when you do express thanks to your Healer, your Provider, your Helper, He is moved to respond and do even more for you.

> *Then he said to him, "Rise and go; your faith has made you well."*
> —Luke 17:19, NIV

Jesus was pleased with this man's grit, and it caused him to do even more for the grateful man. The healed leper's gratitude opened the door for Jesus to go beyond a physical healing. Many commentaries reveal that the man experienced a healing in his soul when Jesus said, "Your faith has made you well." His gratitude led to a deeper level of healing, not only for his body but also for his spirit.

This is an example for us of how we should champion and parent our children. Be encouraged to thank God for answering prayers and the ways He is working in your family. As you show gratitude, God will respond to your grateful heart and do an even greater work, just like He did for the grateful leper.

If I were to give a grateful prayer right now, I could say, "Thank you, God, that Charlie is loving school. Thank You that she is making friends. Thank You that she is learning to read and is making progress in her speech. Thank You that You have gifted her to this family. Thank You for the miracles You have done in her body, and thank You that You aren't done yet."

What does your grateful prayer sound like today? When you pause and think about how God is answering your prayers and meeting the needs of your family, what can you thank Him for? Or, while you are waiting for the answer to your prayers, what else can you see God doing that deserves some expressed gratitude?

Gratitude opens the door for God to work in even more ways in our lives. Don't be like the nine lepers who missed the opportunity to show gratitude and experience a deeper work. Show some grit so that God might do even greater things for your child and in your family!

Showcase God's Goodness

When we express our gratitude, not only can it result in a greater work from the Lord but it also shows His goodness to others. King David showcased the goodness of God throughout the Psalms he wrote. Read how he described the goodness of God in Psalm 145:4–7 (NIV):

One generation commends your works to another;
  they tell of your mighty acts.
They speak of the glorious splendor of your majesty—
  and I will meditate on your wonderful works.
They tell of the power of your awesome works—
  and I will proclaim your great deeds.
They celebrate your abundant goodness
  and joyfully sing of your righteousness.

David knew how to shift his focus to the bigger picture of God's power and awesome works. He loved to celebrate God's goodness and the wonderful things God had done from generation to generation. David definitely had grit that kept him going. Even in some of his darkest times, he expressed thankfulness and reminded himself of who God was and what He had done. In truth, that grit of gratitude is what helped David make it through those dark times.

So many times, I am quick to express my concerns for Charlie. Just recently Charlie had a routine visit to the ear, nose, and throat doctor. The doctor had discovered that Charlie had significant hearing loss in her left ear. I was nervous about more testing and didn't want Charlie to have to have surgery again to get tubes put in her ears. I quickly reached out to family to express our concerns and ask for prayer. Our family responded with encouraging words and prayed for Charlie and for her hearing to come back.

When we returned a month later, Charlie's hearing was back to normal, and the doctor said she didn't need tubes. She was healed! I was so thankful, but I failed to do something so important. It took me several days to give the family the update and celebrate what God had done. I was not as quick to share my gratitude as I was to share the need. As God worked in and through her to bring improvement and healing, I forgot to do what David did, to "proclaim [His] great deeds" and "celebrate [His] abundant goodness."

Lord, let me be just as quick to showcase Your goodness as I am to ask for Your help.

It is good and right to ask others to pray for and with us, but let's also remember to celebrate God's goodness with family and friends as we see Him working in our children.

Look for the Three Ps

If you have a hard time finding things to be grateful for when it comes to your child, let me encourage you with Job 37:14: "Stop and consider God's wonders" (NIV). This Bible verse was printed on a small white card that I kept in my wallet when I was a little girl. As I continue to study the Scriptures and the story of Job, knowing that he was a blessed man who was stripped of his wealth, his health, his loved ones—to consider all that he lost, the pain and suffering he experienced—that verse means even more to me now. Sometimes life gets so hard, and it can be difficult to find things to be grateful for. But we need to do what Job did. We need to slow ourselves down and get ourselves quiet and focus on God's work and wonders.

Stop and take a moment right now to consider the wonderful things God is doing in and through your child. Think about what they can do today that they couldn't do a year ago, or even six months ago. Think about the gifts and passions you see growing inside of them.

If this kind of thankful reflection does not come naturally to you, here are some ways I've worked to intentionally develop more grit so I can see the good, even when life gets challenging. It takes an overcoming, rising above, champion kind of parent to see the positive, the progress, and the potential in our children, and becoming that kind of parent requires discipline. Let's take a look at each of these three Ps as we seek to develop some greater grit.

Positives

Are you someone who naturally focuses on the positive, or would you consider yourself more of a realist, even a pessimist, who sees the negative in situations and circumstances?

In the summer of 2020, Luke and I began to hunt for a new home. We hoped to live on a larger piece of property with more options to meet the needs of our growing family. With our budget and the state of the housing market, many homes we walked into were not picture-perfect, move-in ready, updated, or stylish. Because we were looking at land and location, it forced us to consider older, outdated homes. In all our searching, we learned to develop an eye for the positive. Rather than seeing the old carpet, funky wallpaper, and dated light fixtures, we chose to focus on things like a great floor plan, a spacious backyard, and a home with character that we could make our own. We looked for the positive, and we were able to find a great home that not only met our needs but exceeded our expectations!

We need to focus on God's work and wonders.

In the same way, when we look at our children, rather than focusing on the negative and challenging areas we are facing, we can choose to look for the positive. Instead of dwelling on the discouraging and difficult aspects of parenting a child with special needs, we can take notice of what is rare and beautiful about the precious gift with which God has blessed us.

What a transformation this outlook makes, not only in the way we view our child but also in the way others view them and even how they view themselves. Our children encounter a lot of people, and as they get older, their peers won't always respond positively to them. By noticing the positive, speaking encouragement to our children, and celebrating who they are and what they can do, we can instill in them a stronger sense of confidence and security.

Progress

Every step forward in any area is huge for kids with special needs. The progress our children make will most likely be much slower and harder to see compared to a typical child, but when we step back and consider their progress over time, we can be grateful to God for how far they've come.

Every year when we have an IEP at Charlie's school, I sit down with a team of special education staff and teachers to discuss Charlie's academics. As we make goals and revisit them throughout the year, Charlie's pace (which is usually slower than I expected or hoped) and lack of progress can discourage me. But when we review her IEP again after a full year has gone by, I can see the bigger picture of her development and overall growth. Even if she didn't meet every goal, we can celebrate that she is moving forward and making progress.

Our children are working hard to overcome physical, emotional, and cognitive impairments—we need take time to recognize and be thankful for their progress. When we see the progress, we can be grateful and be a better champion for them.

Potential

And, oh, the potential. The potential we can see in our children is priceless. What do you see in your child that others may not see just yet? What passions and abilities has God put on the inside of them? What potential is in your child? A small seed planted in the ground, when nurtured and cared for, can become a beautiful tree. What may not look like much now can become something great in the future. Zechariah 4:10 (NLT) says, "Do not despise these small beginnings." What seems simple and small now can potentially be something or someone that makes a lasting impact. Remember the historical figures we looked at in the previous chapter? John Wesley, George Washington, Billy Graham—I imagine their beginnings may have seemed small, but they had parents who prayed and who saw their potential.

There is no limit to what God can do in and through our children. Don't despise the present; instead, celebrate the potential. This is just the beginning! God is not done with your child! God loves to take the small things of this world and make them great so that He can show his glory (1 Corinthians 1:27).

Jimmy Evans is an incredible writer, speaker, and marriage and family expert. In his book *Mountaintop of Marriage: A Vision Retreat Guidebook*, he encourages parents to sit down and discuss each of their children, to look at each child and take note of how God has uniquely designed them—their talents, their interests, their personality, and so on. The book guides readers through a series of questions to recognize the positive and potential inside of each child.

When Luke and I did this for each of our three children, I was amazed at what we could see when we actually took time to stop and consider how God had made them. It was fun to talk about each child's unique traits and how they are developing into little people with big personalities. We loved imagining the potential impact they could have on the world and what the future might hold for each of them. Have you ever taken time to sit down and think about your child's giftings and God-given abilities? I encourage you to do this, whether it's through the full Jimmy Evans retreat experience or just a conversation discussing the unique and beautiful way God has made each of your children. Look at your child's potential and thank God for it! Recognizing what makes them special can fill us with hope and help us parent with a greater perspective and level of gratitude.

Get up Grateful

Let's get practical. Our ability to champion for our children with the grit of gratitude won't happen by accident. We need to intentionally create new patterns and ways of thinking to make gratitude a part of our championing.

Rick Warren, pastor of Saddleback Church in Lake Forest, California, has many great teachings on prayer. One of his teachings that has stuck with me is his encouragement to Christians to develop the discipline of prayer throughout the day. He inspires Christians to have an ongoing prayer life that doesn't start and stop in the morning but lasts throughout the day.

His advice? *Get up grateful.* Start the day expressing your gratitude to God. Before you even get out of bed, start telling God what you are grateful for.

The challenge to get up grateful has stuck with me. How important it is to wake up in the morning with a grateful heart and say, "God, I am grateful that You are drawing me to You today. I am grateful that I have breath in my lungs. I am thankful to wake up next to my husband. I am thankful that I have another day to worship You. Thank You for another day to love my family."

Our grateful prayers might look and sound different from one person to another, but we can all get practical and implement this habit into our daily lives. It is a great way to live out 1 Thessalonians 5:17–18 (NKJV): "In everything give thanks; for this is the will of God in Christ Jesus for you."

Gratitude Is Good for You

As we champion for our children, the grit of gratitude can go a long way. It helps us see the bigger picture of how God is working, it opens doors for God to do an even greater work, it showcases His goodness, and it can change our outlook on life. And finally, the grit of gratitude is honestly good for us! Proverbs 17:22 says, "A happy heart is good medicine and a joyful mind causes healing..." (Amplified Bible). When we are grateful, we are happy. Happiness is like good medicine for our souls. The grit of gratitude will set you apart as a parent who chooses to be thankful and lives a life of overcoming. Gratitude won't just impact your child and your ability to champion for them, but it will also directly affect your mind, your heart, and your ability to enjoy life and experience happiness.

In our next chapter, we will see how God gives us a great promise that will carry us as we champion for our children, a promise that makes the future bright and full of hope for both our children and for us. It is a promise that I have held close to my heart for many years.

Chapter 7
Strength to Strength

They go from strength to strength.

—Psalm 84:7, NIV

At the University of Arizona, scientists have created something called Biosphere 2, which is a mini version of our planet. With this tiny earth model, scientists have been able to study plant life, among other things, and gain new insights into how our planet's living systems work.

One particular study gave them a greater understanding of the importance of wind to a tree. Trees planted in Biosphere 2 grew more rapidly compared to typical trees planted and growing in unprotected, natural surroundings. Although these trees grew quickly, they failed to develop into full maturity. They collapsed because their bark wasn't strong enough to support their structure. One thing the Biosphere 2 didn't provide was something very common in nature—wind. Without wind, the trees couldn't develop reaction wood (stress wood) that provides the strength a tree needs to reach its greatest growth potential.

When trees grow in nature, they must constantly adapt and adjust to the wind. As they adjust, this special type of reaction wood, which has a different cellulose structure and lignin content, develops, making the tree strong and able to mature. The more stress the wind causes, the more strength the tree must develop to keep growing.

As parents who are fulfilling our calling to champion, we will face winds—challenges that force us to adjust, adapt, and develop strength.

Just like the impact on the tree, challenges can help us become better. The stress won't weaken us; on the contrary, it can make us stronger because of Christ in us.

> ... we also glory in our sufferings, because we know that suffering produces perseverance; perseverance, character; and character, hope. And hope does not put us to shame, because God's love has been poured out into our hearts ...
>
> —Romans 5:3–5, NIV

The wind will produce strength in us, and as a result, we will be better able to support and champion our children. We will adapt, learn, grow, and get better with every season. We are on a lifelong journey, but we have the power and strength of God at work inside of us that will bring us to full maturity in Him and lead us from strength to strength.

A Promise of Strength

Our years of rising up and championing come with something special, something that we have been promised each and every day. You may be thinking that the sleepless nights, the early onset of wrinkles, and the constant need for a giant thermos of coffee don't count as *special* in your eyes. But I'm not talking about those things. For all who believe in Christ and choose to put their trust in Him, He has given a promise that will carry them through every season and challenge they might face as a family.

There are many things we don't know as parents. We don't know what the future will bring for our children, especially our children with special needs. We believe and pray for God's supernatural work and favor to be at work in their lives, but we don't know what tomorrow will look like.

I often imagine what the future will hold for Charlie. I wonder what high school will look like and what academic and social obstacles she will have to face. I wonder what her adolescent years will hold—liking boys, wanting her independence, her interest in fashion and makeup. I wonder what she will want to do when she graduates, if she will be driven and focused or need some extra time to explore her interests. I wonder where her adult years will lead her. Will she get a higher-level education? Will she find a job she loves? Will she live at home with us, or be ready for something new? I don't have the answers to any of these questions. Yes, I have dreams and prayers, but the future remains a mystery until we take those days head-on and walk into those moments together.

With each of those days and moments that await, there is one thing we can know: We know we each have been given a promise—a promise for today, and the next day, and the next day. In Deuteronomy 33:25 (NKJV), we are promised, "As your days, so shall your strength be." No matter what the day holds, the Lord has promised strength. He will give physical, mental, spiritual, and emotional strength. We have been given a promise for daily strength as we trust the Lord and abide in Him. We can find great peace in this promise. We don't need to worry about the future; rather, we can live fully in the present and depend upon the Lord for the strength He has given us for today. He keeps His promises, and He is sovereign.

We can live fully in the present and depend upon the Lord for the strength He has given us for today.

Easton's Bible Dictionary defines the sovereignty of God as His "absolute right to do all things according to his own good pleasure." What does this mean for us? God is in control, and He has the power to sustain and carry our family to accomplish His good purpose. He is able to supply us with the strength we need to parent each and every day. As our days are, so shall our strength be. As time goes on and we continue to rely on and trust God, we won't get more and more tired, burned out, or have to quit. He will give us the supply of strength we need for the day and the season we are in with our children because He has sovereignly chosen and equipped us to champion for our children.

My friend, if you trust Him, you won't get weaker. You won't be overcome. You will remain strong in the Lord. And if you find yourself wrestling with thoughts of hopelessness or fear, realize those thoughts are not from the Lord. When you find yourself getting weary from the day-in and day-out of parenting your child with special needs and your strength tank is running low, remember the promise. The Lord has given us a promise of strength that we can hold on to. Rise up in the strong power God has put inside of you. Set your heart on Him. Call out to God who is sovereign and who promises to equip you for every season you face with your child.

Strong Power

Charlie has a saying right now that is timely for this challenge we face and the promise we need to take hold of. Any time she does something that requires extra strength, like riding her bike a long distance or crossing the monkey bars all by herself, she completes the task, flexes her biceps, and declares, "I've got strong power!" She says it with such passion that we can't help but smile. "I've got strong power!" *Yes, Honey, you do! There is strength inside of you that can help you accomplish and conquer things you didn't know you could.*

And to you, friend, I say the same! The strength God will place inside you each day is a strong power that will carry you and sustain you for all your days!

> *And if the Spirit of him who raised Jesus from the dead is living in you, he who raised Christ from the dead will also give life to your mortal bodies because of his Spirit who lives in you.*
> —Romans 8:11, NIV

That strong power, described in Romans 8:11, goes beyond human effort and striving. It is a supernatural strength that can unfold in our lives, causing others to see Jesus and be drawn to Him. There is strong power that God has placed within you, fellow champion. Be confident in it and use that strong power to fulfill your calling and be who God created you to be!

As you allow the strength of God to work in and through you, you can be confident that He who began a good work in you will carry it out to completion (Philippians 1:6). You will be able to finish your race and champion until the end. You will have the strength to pray and hold on to His promises. You will have the strength to make decisions. You will be able to rise up with strong power because God has chosen you to champion for your child, and His strength will carry you to the end.

1% Philosophy

The Ironman race is for the most determined of athletes. The physical and mental strength it takes to endure a 2.4-mile swim, a 112-mile bike ride, and a 26.2-mile run is incredible. For forty-two years, thousands of the most physically fit and mentally strong athletes have participated in this event. Athletes need a full day to complete all portions of the race and must cross the finish line under seventeen hours. And for twenty-one-year-old Chris Nikic, those standards still applied, even though Chris was born with Down syndrome.

Chris is a young man from Maitland, Florida, who set out to become the first athlete with Down syndrome to compete in this iconic race. Though Chris had his share of developmental delays as a child, he was determined to overcome the challenges of his disability and the negativity he often faced from others growing up. Though Chris still struggles with balance, slow reaction time, and low muscle tone, he hasn't stopped running toward his goals to achieve his dreams. Chris simply believes, "It's easy to be successful because I only need to get 1 percent better each day."

Before participating in the Ironman race in November of 2020, Chris was an athlete in the Special Olympics. Completing the 1000-meter, open-water lake swim in a Special Olympics triathlon inspired him to seek out greater challenges. "Chris World Champ," as he titled himself, began the hard work to prepare for the Ironman, a race few athletes have the courage or mental stamina to participate in. Chris' determination to get 1 percent better each day carried him through months of training as he juggled school, homework, and thirty hours of workouts each week. In 2020, Chris' greatest accomplishment was celebrated at a national level when he not only competed in the Ironman but was the first athlete with Down syndrome to complete every mile of swimming, biking, and running.

His 1 percent philosophy has been key to his ability to persevere and accomplish what he sets out to do! Chris now gives motivational speeches to young people around the world. He has become a hero and example to many athletes and offers hope and inspiration to families who are raising a child with Down syndrome.

Much like Chris' philosophy of getting better little by little, we can take a similar approach as we champion for our children. With the promises God has given us and the power that is at work inside of us, we will get stronger as our children get older. We will be able to walk into the future with confidence because God is helping us grow so that we can fulfill our purpose in Him.

Strength to Strength

This promise of strength is also given to our children. Several years ago, I found myself becoming weary as a mother. I felt like I was praying the same prayers over and over for my children and not seeing the results I wanted, particularly for Charlie. I was losing vision and passion in my prayers. I was needing God to refresh and strengthen me as a mother and renew my hope for Charlie.

As I sat next to my husband one Sunday morning at church, the message was coming to an end, and, like many times, the pastor invited people to come forward for prayer during the final worship song. Charlie was heavy on my heart, so when the invitation came, I stood up without hesitation and walked toward the pastor. I had only been there for a moment when God impressed on my heart the words "strength to strength." I immediately felt my heart strengthen, and I knew how I needed to pray for Charlie. I needed to pray and believe that she would go from strength to strength and that her progress wasn't over but would continue. His words filled me with hope that, although we weren't seeing results and answers to our prayers yet, God was sure to keep working. That day I began to pray that Charlie would go from strength to strength—physically, emotionally, cognitively, and spiritually. And as I prayed that promise, I was able to move forward with purpose and passion.

This promise, that we and our children will go from strength to strength, is found in the Psalms.

> *Blessed are those whose strength is in you, whose hearts are set on pilgrimage. As they pass through the Valley of Baka, they make it a place of springs; the autumn rains also cover it with pools. They go from strength to strength . . .*
>
> —Psalm 84:5–7, NIV

We are on a pilgrimage as parents. This is a long road and a high calling. I don't know where you are in the journey. Your children may be young like mine, teenagers, or adults. But if you draw your strength from God and set your heart on Him and His calling for your life, He will equip you for every step. You will be able to pass through valleys (challenges and difficult times), and there you will experience refreshing and refilling (springs and rains). You will go from strength to strength.

The moment I took hold of the promise in Psalm 84, I felt renewed in my vision to champion for Charlie. I stood on that promise of strength for my daughter and for myself, and I have seen the hand and power of God moving in our family ever since. We still go through valleys, but we rely on God's promise to be with us. With Him, we will go from strength to strength.

The Creator Still Creates

In the realm of advocacy and championing for our children, some areas require more faith and effort on our part than others. I find it easy to advocate for Charlie in prayer when it comes to the day-to-day things, like protection at school, favor with teachers, and the wisdom to make decisions for her health and development. I see God answer these prayers repeatedly, so my faith and confidence are strong when I pray these types of championing prayers.

But then there have been those big things we have had to pray and believe for that required big faith. These things seemed out of reach, and, if I'm being honest, my momma mind doubted the outcome. In these seasons, I have had to dig deeper to pray in spite of that doubt.

One of those times was when we needed a financial miracle to be able to pay off the medical bills that piled up when Charlie had multiple surgeries, doctor visits, and lab tests in a short span. That year, it felt like we were addressing all the major health issues that come with Trisomy 21 at once. We didn't have enough in our checking account to pay the medical bills, and dipping that deep into our savings would have put too much financial stress on our family.

I just didn't see how God was going to provide and give us the miracle we needed. But as we passed through that valley and put our trust in God, rain came. Checks came in the mail—the state granted our requests for financial assistance, and people blessed our family financially without even knowing our need at the time. God brought the rain in the valley and led us from strength to strength.

Another time I had to pray through doubt was when the doctor told us that Charlie would need braces for her feet and ankles until the age of ten. Down syndrome causes low muscle tone, and the doctor told us her muscles just weren't strong enough to help her walk properly. The way her legs and hips were compensating for her lack of ligament strength was going to cause her to need support from braces for several years. So many kids her age had braces, and it seemed like my only option was to accept the fact that Charlie would need braces as well, just as the doctor said. But I chose to rise up and champion in prayer. We asked family and friends to pray and believe for healing with us. And again, as we passed through that valley, God healed Charlie. She has been without braces since she was four years old! God took Charlie from strength to strength!

～

I just didn't see how God was going to provide and give us the miracle we needed.

～

The same thing happened when doctors told us that Charlie would always have digestive issues and need medicine every day to help her system process and pass food properly. This is another typical challenge for individuals with Down syndrome. But we wanted to believe that God would heal Charlie and show His glory through strengthening her digestive system. After adjusting her diet, working with Charlie, and praying for healing, she no longer needs to take medicine. Because God gave us wisdom and healed her body, Charlie still has a healthy digestive system.

These are just a few of the big things that we believed God for as we prayed that He would provide, heal, and meet us in these valleys. He has been so faithful to provide springs, bring the rain, and give us strength.

Maybe you're like me. You find it easy to have hope and believe God for the day-to-day needs of your child, but when it comes the big things, you aren't sure your faith is big enough or that our God is big enough. Let me encourage you with a truth from Ephesians 3:20: God can do even more than we ask or imagine, according to his power (or strength) that is at work in us. Not only can God answer your prayers, but He is able to do above and beyond what you are asking.

There is a scripture that Charlie's grandma believes and prays for her that gives me so much confidence in what God can do. God is not limited by what we can see or perceive. He can create something out of nothing and perform a miracle in our valley.

> *You have heard; now see all this; and will you not declare it? From this time forth I announce to you new things, hidden things that you have not known. They are created now, not long ago; before today you have never heard of them . . .*
>
> —Isaiah 48:6–7, ESV

This scripture tells us that God is not only the One who created but He is *still creating* today! God created and formed your child, but He is not limited to the original template. He can create even now!

Even though your child was born with a physical or cognitive impairment, God can still create, form, and do new things. He can create the muscle, activate dormant parts of the brain, and open the pathways of communication and language. Knowing the Creator isn't done and can do more even now can fill us with hope to champion, even in the valley.

Oh, let us believe! The One who is still creating is not limited by doctors' or teachers' evaluations and predictions for our children. He is not limited by what you see in your bank account. He can create and provide because that is what He does! He is the same yesterday and today and forever (Hebrews 13:8), and He can create even now.

Strength Paradox

As Christians, we are living our lives within a *strength paradox*. A paradox is something seemingly absurd that when explained may prove to be true. The idea of a strength paradox comes from 2 Corinthians 12:10. This scripture says that when we are weak, we are strong. Yes, you read that right. My weakness paves the way toward strength. Being weak is the first step to becoming strong.

This is good news for us! On our worst days, when we are feeling tired, worn out, and overwhelmed, that's when the strength of God is even more at work in our lives. This truth is found in the scripture right before the verse above:

> *But he said to me, "My grace is sufficient for you, for my power is made perfect in weakness." Therefore I will boast all the more gladly of my weaknesses, so that the power of Christ may rest upon me. For the sake of Christ, then, I am content with weaknesses, insults, hardships, persecutions, and calamities. For when I am weak, then I am strong.*
>
> *—2 Corinthians 12:9–10, ESV*

When we are in a place of weakness, God's strength can be at work in us, enabling us to do and be more than we can on our own. Our weakness opens the door for His strength to be at work in our lives. Don't hide your weaknesses from God; share them with Him so that His promise to bring power and strength can meet you in your valley.

Step into Strength

Let's step into the promise of His strength today. May we carry this prayer of going from strength to strength in our hearts. As I believe for Charlie, I will also believe for you and your child, that we will all go from strength to strength. There is no limit to God's power and what He can do in our lives. Let's choose to trust in His power and His promises. If we choose to be champions for our children, with the help of God, we can thrive with the strength God provides. Remember that you have strong power inside you as you surrender to Christ. He can create and give strength even in the weakest areas and the deepest valleys. So, let's champion together with the strength of Christ at work within each of us and our children.

Chapter 8
Advocate Allies Part 1— Parents and Ministry Leaders

Plans fail for lack of counsel, but with many advisers they succeed.

—Proverbs 15:22, NIV

We are never alone in this journey. We've seen promises of God's presence and strength in the past few chapters. He also provides other people to join us as we champion for our children. As you consider all the families, professionals, teachers, and doctors who have crossed your path, know that they all represent opportunities for better advocacy. We can join forces with these many advisors and potentially have greater success championing for our children because of the knowledge and resources they offer.

It may feel, at times, that we are fighting against systems and structures, but that fight also gives us an opportunity to gain wisdom from those we respect and admire who are leaders in the areas where our children need greater support and expertise. We can choose to gain insight and fight with these individuals to advocate for our children. They can become our allies.

Through the years, I have had the honor of connecting with amazing parents, ministry leaders, teachers, and doctors who have all been willing to share wisdom from their experience in championing for children with special needs. These leaders have so much knowledge to share that I have chosen to break down our advocate ally information into two parts.

In this first part, we will gain insight from fellow parents who are championing for their children within their communities. They will share what they have learned about successful advocacy through the experiences they have had with their child. We will also hear from ministry leaders. With church being such a large part of our lives, I sought out advice from children's ministry leaders who can help us better understand our role in helping our children find their place within church and ministry settings. I am excited to share with you what I think is very valuable counsel that can help us and our children succeed.

I know that helpful opinions and experiences go beyond these pages and those I asked to share, so I encourage you to gather counsel from those you know as well. We can become better champions when we are open to advice from others and when we have teachable hearts. As we gather wisdom from many advisors, my hope is that these words will encourage you and give you greater confidence to help your child thrive.

Parent Allies

I want to start off by introducing an amazing mother who advocates for her daughter with an incredible passion that is contagious.

Jen is mother to Addie and her three younger siblings. Addie is sixteen years old and has Down syndrome. She is currently in high school. Jen's family is kind and full of love for one another and people. The pictures of their life in sunny California posted on social media always make me envious of their warm weather, especially during our cold, gray days here in Michigan.

I found Jen one day while I was looking up conferences offered to mothers of children with special needs, specifically Down syndrome. One of those conferences takes place on the other side of the country, in Laguna Beach, California. The Dear Mom Conference is a beautiful event created to connect with and pour into mothers. While searching for the details of this event, I came across the lineup of featured speakers.

I was curious who these Dear Mom Conference speakers were and what their stories were all about. Looking into Jen and her story as a mom, I felt compelled to reach out. Thanks to social media, it's easy to connect and meet new people, so I sent Jen a message. She was kind enough to respond and do a FaceTime chat, and we have stayed connected ever since. She mentors me from afar as I watch her love God and her family. Jen uses her voice to strengthen others in many ways, but I have been most impacted by her voice as a champion for Addie.

With Addie being her firstborn (just like our Charlie), and with all the wisdom and experience she has as a mother, I have found Jen to be a great ally in championing for my children. Here are a few thoughts from Jen:

> The greatest obstacle in advocacy is dealing with other people's limiting beliefs. Helping educate others about the possibilities for my child—helping them see that proper resources and access to general education and social environments is the best-case scenario for Addie and others—has been the most frustrating piece to navigate.
>
> To successfully advocate, you must be kind, but don't take no for an answer. When it comes to advocating for my child for extracurricular activities, I like to meet with leaders of the community event or activity to give them time to find the support they need to see my child included. I communicate with confidence that her participation is appropriate and that we will come alongside to support her as necessary. However, leaning into her strengths, just like you would with any other child, will enable success for her and the rest of the team or community. Then I have to be okay with her participation looking a little modified.
>
> If you want to start making a difference in your community as an advocate, you should start by being a friend. Always be learning people's first language and treating them like anyone else you desire connection with. Understand that you likely do not know all they carry. The fear of rejection and pain is real, so feel free to ask questions and not assume you know.
>
> In advocacy, I have learned not to come off too strong out the gate. Taking a posture as a part of the team instead of an adversary is best.

Champion for Charlie

> We treat Addie like the rest of our four kids. She fully participates in the activities we do. She attends her age-appropriate church program. She has sleepovers with her cousins and engages in game nights and other extra-fun events with our family. She has volunteered at church and served at community events like feeding the homeless. She plays sports at her local high school and engages in all the fun events and camps with support. She has her own social media account and shares parts of her life with my oversight.

I am so thankful for fellow parents like Jen who will share from their experiences. Her wisdom helps me better champion for Charlie. And hopefully her words are helpful for you as well! Although your approach or perspective might be different, you can still become allies with respected and loving parents like Jen and learn a lot!

Another hero ally, Pam, is dear to my heart. Pam was the first person to speak into my life as a fellow mother raising a child with Trisomy 21. Pam is the mother of Geoff, who is now a thirty-eight-year-old man with Down syndrome. When Pam spoke words of hope and healing to my heart as a young mother, I was set on a new path. I know Pam's words and wisdom will be a great blessing to you:

> I must say that Geoff's greatest advocate all these years has been our Savior, Jesus Christ. As we have prayed over his programs, teachers, friends, respite care providers, therapists, and even bus drivers, God has been so faithful to bring into his life the most wonderful, caring people. The medical field would be the one area where I've felt the need to press in more and advocate on Geoff's behalf.
>
> I remember that my OB/GYN at the time of Geoff's birth was so grieved as he told me the "bad news" about our baby. The nurses rushed me off to a private room down the corridor at the hospital and treated me like something horrible had happened to me. I was so confused as they brought me this tiny bundle of joy because they were so quiet and seemed so sad for me.

Geoff's pediatrician, however, had a very different attitude. He was so encouraging! He challenged me to try to help make the situation different in that hospital for the next set of new parents.

Not too many months after Geoff was born, I met another mom with a baby a year older than Geoff who had Downs, and together we began a support group to try to graciously educate the doctors and nurses at the hospital on how better to help new parents. We also provided packets of positive, up-to-date information about Down syndrome for new parents.

Even today, we can still encounter new doctors who seem like they are uncomfortable with Geoff or do not display the same value for his quality of life as we do. My husband and I both try to go to Geoff's doctors' appointments, and we have found consistently that it doesn't take very long for that type of attitude in a doctor to change. As they pick up on our love and care for this young man, it seems they, too, change their disposition and treat Geoff with the finest of care.

As an adult, Geoff still makes some weird noises, and he likes to talk a lot. His speech is hard for someone new to understand. Younger children will sometimes stare at him. In those kinds of situations, we always try to introduce Geoff and help others see and understand and get to know him a little better right on the spot. As we take the gracious approach of giving others the benefit of the doubt and realizing it is our privilege to help others get to know and be blessed by our kiddos, others are blessed! And then they become a blessing to us and especially to our child.

Our beautiful children are created in the image of God. How blessed we are to showcase His love and grace and mercy toward each person that comes into our child's life, knowing that our child may just be the one to point the way to our Great Advocate, our beautiful Savior, Jesus Christ!

After years of parenting, Pam's heart has only become softer toward others, more thankful, and more aware of God working in and through her child. I want a heart like that. When my Charlie is an adult, I want to look at her with the same kind of love and awe at what God has done and show the same grace toward others.

We can form allies with parents at every step of our championing journey. Some we will agree with, and some we may not. Some will inspire us, and others will be inspired by us. The goal is to take advantage of the opportunity we have among these fellow champions. Don't journey alone. Reach out—send that email or message, make that phone call—and create connections with parent allies you respect and want to learn from.

Ministry Leader Allies

As I mentioned earlier, an important part of our parenting is taking our children to church. Within weeks of having each of my children, we headed back to Sunday morning and midweek services. With my husband being a pastor and our love for the local church, I was anxious to get back to my church family and community. And as Charlie has grown up in the church, there have been adjustments, adaptations, and several conversations to help her and the staff have the best experience possible. This has been a learning curve for me, and I'm continuing to navigate my way through this area of championing for my daughter, which is why having allies can be so helpful!

I also include this aspect of ally advocacy because I have found that many parents have fears or have had negative experiences taking their child with special needs to church. They are concerned about the setting their child will be in, aware of the potential for overstimulation, or unsure about the safety or the structures in place. They are concerned about volunteers and staff who will be working with their child, whether they will have adequate knowledge, experience, or demonstrate confidence in various scenarios. Parents wonder if their family and their child will feel accepted or feel unwelcomed since they may not look like the typical families who attend the church.

I want to introduce to you a wonderful mother and ministry leader who also happens to have a beautiful adult daughter with special needs.

Advocate Allies Part 1—Parents and Ministry Leaders

When I spoke with Heather, she was serving as the Buddy Break coordinator in a local church. Buddy Break is one of the many ministries offered through a national organization known as Nathaniel's Hope, which strives to bring help and hope to those who desperately need it. Heather opened the doors of their church to children with special needs, along with their siblings, every month to offer a safe, loving environment to experience the love of Jesus. It's an opportunity that also allows these children's parents to get a much-needed break. Here are a few of Heather's thoughts on how to successfully champion for your child in ministry settings:

> It is important for parents and ministry leaders to work together to ensure that the child has a good experience during programming. Parents should be open and honest with information regarding the child's abilities, sensitivities, triggers, and preferences. This will allow the staff to be prepared for behaviors that may occur and to also have activities, fidgets, etc. available that the child likes.
>
> We have seen parents drop off kids and hope that no one will notice. It is better for the parent to be proactive and talk with ministry staff about their child to better equip the staff. Parents should not drop off their child without informing the ministry staff of their child's needs. It's also helpful if they keep drop-off brief and not linger too long. Kids can sense that their parents are still there and may not engage as well.
>
> It's helpful to give reassurance to the parents that it may take several attempts before the child wants to stay. It can take many visits and contacts for the child to feel comfortable, adapt to the situation, and get to know the routine and expectations of the programming. They should have patience and understand that it will take time for their child to feel comfortable. It also helps if they are consistent in attendance. Attending once in a while does not build a routine for the child.
>
> The parents should speak with the ministry department about their child's specific needs and how they would function during programming. This could be done via phone before

their first time at church. We also have invited families to come into the church at a time outside of a Sunday morning so that they can experience the setting without the usual busyness. Regarding types of communication, any form of contact that works best for the family is good, including phone calls, face-to-face meetings, or a scheduled time outside of Sundays. We tailor it to the needs of the family.

As ministry volunteers, we love to come alongside parents, siblings, and the child with special needs. We realize that the journey can be difficult and often lonely. We try to build a relationship and get to know the entire family. It has been so fun to watch our kids grow and develop.

Heather offers great advice. As parents, sometimes we overcomplicate things. We just need to start the conversations, voice our concerns, and ask some questions.

Heather's ministry specifically focuses on children with special needs within the church setting. Now I would like you to hear from another church leader who oversees an entire children's ministry.

Becky leads the children's ministry at our home church, Cornerstone Church, in Highland, Michigan. She leads a full team of volunteer teachers on a weekly basis and oversees the discipleship and experience of hundreds of children within her ministry. Here's what our ally says about working together with parents to ensure a child with special needs can have a positive experience at church:

> The parent of a special-needs child should partner with ministry leaders by allowing their kids to attend classes, services, and special events offered by the children's ministry. If parents have concerns about their child's engagement in class, they are welcome to talk to their child's teacher before or after class or schedule a phone call with me to address their concerns.
>
> In general, face-to-face communication is preferred. If the parent is concerned that their child's needs may be more than the church can handle, they are welcome to call me at the church office ahead of time.

A parent should not hold back truthful information about their child. I have had many parents place their child in a class at church and say nothing about them even having special needs. Most of the time, it seems to come from a desire to have their child treated as "normal," which I can understand, but we are a discipleship ministry, and it helps the team more effectively disciple if the needs are readily made known.

The relationship between the parent and the child's teacher is a partnership to disciple children to be followers of Christ. When a parent decides to join a particular local church, they choose the church's pastor as a shepherd for the hearts of their family, including the hearts of their children. Children's Sunday school teachers are an extension of the pastor's spiritual authority in the life of every child who attends. When a parent allows a Sunday school teacher to contribute to shaping the soul of their child, it requires trust. The Sunday school teacher must be worthy of the parents' trust and transparent about what is being taught in the classroom.

The parents are the biggest spiritual influencers in a child's life. The children's ministry team supports and helps to advance the spiritual discipleship that is primarily implemented by the parent. Parents cannot abdicate their spiritual authority over their child to the Sunday school teacher but must fulfill their responsibility to raise their child in the ways of the Lord.

When we reach out to potential allies in ministry, our children can have a better experience at church. Church doesn't have to be avoided or overcomplicated. Just as you champion for your child among your family, with their schoolteacher, or with doctors, you can do the same within the church. Don't shy away from taking your family to church because of one bad experience. Don't assume the worst and be selective in your championing platforms. Don't give up on what is possible, not only for your child's sake but for the sake of others with special needs as well. Everyone in your family can find their place in church. It just might take a little extra effort to make it happen.

Champion Challenge

I hope you have found this parent and ministry leader wisdom helpful for you and your child. There are many things we have yet to experience, and it's helpful to hear from those who are further along in the journey. Here are some of the tips we can take away from what they've shared:

Ally Advice from Parents

1. Help educate others.
2. Be kind and communicate with confidence.
3. Make a difference in your community by being a friend first and learning to care for others and their story.
4. Gather teammates, not adversaries.
5. Treat your child with special needs the same as your other children.
6. Trust that God is advocating for your child.
7. Use what you learn from your negative experiences to improve the experiences of those who come after you.
8. Lead by example to show others how they should respond to your child.
9. Be gracious and take advantage of opportunities to teach others how to engage with your child.

Ally Advice from Ministry Leaders

1. Work together with ministry leaders and be honest about your child's needs.
2. Be proactive and help equip the ministry staff.
3. Know that it will take more than one visit to church for your child and their teachers to get comfortable with one another.
4. Create time to communicate with ministry leaders (phone call, face-to-face meeting, visiting the church outside of regular service times).
5. Build meaningful relationships with leaders.

6. Trust your child's ministry leader and the decisions they will make for your child.
7. Remember that you should be the primary spiritual influence in your child's life and that the ministry is there to offer support through a positive partnership.

I hope these advocate allies have encouraged you to begin conversations and champion for your child in new ways. I would challenge you to reach out to fellow parents who are strong champions and advocates. Send a text, grab a coffee, or schedule a playdate with that fellow champion and their kids. Take advantage of the experiences of others and gather their counsel! And if you don't know of anyone in your area, get on social media, do some research, and be brave by sending that email or message. Get the lines of communication open! You may have to try a couple different allies, but if you hear from just one, that's one more than you have right now. Take advantage of their counsel and allow their wisdom to help you help your child succeed.

We've heard great advice from Jen, Pam, Heather, and Becky, and we have much more ahead! I'm really excited for the advocate allies you will hear from in the next chapter. Their experience in the classroom and the medical field will bring clarity to situations we face as we champion for our children.

Chapter 9
Advocate Allies Part 2—Teachers and Doctors

And Jesus grew in wisdom and stature, and in favor with God and man.

—Luke 2:52, NIV

As you've seen in this book, we can pray for our children in many ways and for many reasons. One prayer I have prayed over and over again is inspired by Luke 2:52. When we read about the life of Jesus, we don't find much about His childhood and adolescent years, but we do know that He grew "in wisdom and stature and favor with God and man." So, time and time again, I pray for all three of my children to do just that. *Lord, I pray that Charlie, Owen, and Nora would grow in wisdom and stature and in favor with You and men.*

When it comes to our children growing in these two ways—wisdom and stature—I think about their cognitive and physical development. It is in these two areas that I believe parents can fight their greatest battles for their children. I have shed more tears over Charlie's mental and physical development than any other struggles she has had. Our greatest challenges have been with Charlie's cognitive and physical delays. They can lead to overwhelming stress, frustration, and pain for both child and parent, and much of it can be channeled toward educators and medical professionals. We can feel like they don't fully understand our child, their needs, their potential, or our concerns.

Rather than teachers and doctors being allies, some parents take the opposite perspective and see them as enemies, but I wanted to take the opportunity to start a dialogue with these allies and hear from these individuals who have such a profound impact on my children's development. Who better to join forces with than those who educate my children and oversee their health and well-being? I believe we have the opportunity to become allies with teachers and doctors, so, just as I did with fellow parents and ministry leaders, I set out to ask questions, get perspective, and gain some greater wisdom in how to work with them.

Not every teacher or doctor has your child's best interest in mind. I understand that. But I have reached out to trusted teachers and doctors who have proven their professional expertise, are dedicated to their calling, and have a genuine love for their students and patients. I hope that you find these allies as helpful as I have.

Teacher Allies

We constantly pray for our daughter's teachers. We pray that she will have teachers who fight for her, want to see her succeed, and who truly love her. We pray that they will have wisdom, be creative, and help her meet academic goals. As we have prayed for teachers year after year, I have seen God work on Charlie's behalf. I would love for you to hear from three teachers, all of whom I consider amazing allies.

Mrs. Conroy is an early childhood teacher consultant in the public school system here in Fenton, Michigan. With almost twenty-five years of experience, she was an incredible part of our early years of education and schooling with Charlie. Here are a few thoughts from Mrs. Conroy:

> A relationship between parent and teacher must be built on mutual trust and respect. I believe that when a parent trusts an educator, the relationship is open and honest. Being an educator of very young children, I am often the first school experience they have. I have always made it a priority to make parents feel completely at ease leaving their baby with me. I, in turn, respect the parents by knowing and never forgetting that this child is the light of their world. Sometimes

Advocate Allies Part 2—Teachers and Doctors

parents of very young children are still unsure about what to do with the reality that their child has special needs, so working with families, not just the student, is an important part of my job. We often spend more than one year together. I view these families as my own.

Communication is key. I always work hard at communicating with parents about their child's day at school, about progress, upcoming events, etc. I *love* when I get updates about home life. Follow-through is important too. We have multiple staff working with students, and many will provide ideas for parents. We *love* when parents take the time to follow through with those ideas. Consistency between home and school is so important.

Sending emails or making phone calls when you are emotionally charged can hurt the relationship between parent and teacher. It is always good to wait and reflect a bit on an issue, with the exception of something life-threatening, of course.

Mutual trust between parent and teacher is vital for supporting students. In my experience, teachers have genuine intentions of helping their students. Sometimes hearing something about your child can be taken personally. Choose to change the narrative in your head to, "This teacher is just trying to help."

Opt for face-to-face meetings, as emails can often be misinterpreted. Share your ideas and experiences with what has worked well at home. Again, if there is a relationship built on mutual respect and trust, these types of conversations are much easier.

Regarding an IEP meeting, the paperwork is very intimidating. There are a lot of terms and acronyms in the world of special education. Parents should educate themselves on the process of the IEP. Do not be afraid to ask too many questions. Get to know all the parts of an IEP. Know your rights in the process. In our program, we have always devoted one parent group meeting to going through IEP 101. I think this helps the parents understand the process. Before an IEP, review the previous IEP to help gather information and questions. Although an IEP needs to be reviewed once a year, it does not always need to wait that long. If a student is struggling to achieve goals, set up a meeting with the teacher to review progress.

I believe that parents and teachers are partners. Follow-through and consistency are key when working with young special-needs children.

Mrs. Conroy has been an integral part of Charlie's school experience. She helped us transition Charlie from early intervention to kindergarten, then from kindergarten to elementary school. She also connected me to the next teacher ally I want you to hear from, whose eleven years of experience as an elementary special education teacher for students with mild cognitive impairments has made her a champion among teachers.

Mrs. Gecele has an MEd in special education with a cognitive impairment emphasis and an added endorsement in emotional impairments. She has helped Charlie make progress in ways greater than I imagined were possible. Here are a few thoughts from Mrs. Gecele:

> The educator and parent/caregiver relationship is truly key to a child's success. Within my own classroom family, I not only want parent support—I need it as well. Helping a student grow academically, socially, and behaviorally takes great effort from everyone involved in the child's learning. I truly want parents to partner with me, and a partnership requires positive and respectful communication. Actively asking questions about a child's education and working on assignments at home are both great ways to show a teacher that you believe learning is not just something that happens at school. If a parent disagrees with the methods or strategies being used in the classroom, they should set up a meeting or phone conversation with the teacher. We are fortunate to live in a time when texts and emails can be used for communication, but when there are points of disagreement or concerns

about a child and their learning, in-person or phone conversations are always better options for communicating with a teacher. Instead of a sharp or short criticism of their teaching methodologies, I would suggest asking for more clarification about why they are teaching something a certain way or asking if the teacher has had success in the classroom using the strategies in question.

If a parent feels that their child isn't making progress in a particular area, they should talk to the teacher immediately. The teacher may be able to offer extra practice, suggestions, or other support options outside of school. The parent may also have valuable information about what occurs at home that could be beneficial to the teacher's preparation and lesson teaching.

It is also important to remember that parent behaviors, decisions, and attitudes can make a big difference in a child's success. A child needs to know not only that their parent(s) fully believe their goals are achievable but that they will commit to partnering with the teacher as well.

In preparation for an IEP, it is important to remember that all the members in the IEP make up the team. As a parent, you are an integral part of the team! It is perfectly acceptable, and even recommended, to ask for a draft copy ahead of time to review. This way, if there are concerns or questions, the parent can bring them up prior to the IEP. This benefits the whole team and allows for a much more productive meeting to take place. One question that is important to consider is, *Is my child in their least restrictive environment?* I would also suggest thinking about what your personal goals and wishes are for your child and how those align with what has been put in place for your child's education through their IEP. If those two do not align, then you need to work with your child's teachers so that everyone feels comfortable with and confident in what has been written in the IEP.

Champion for Charlie

Such great advice from both Mrs. Conroy and Mrs. Gecele! I want to share some final insights from a teacher who has been a great resource for me. She is a friend and previous co-worker who supported special-needs students as a paraprofessional in my elementary classroom years ago. Mrs. Salem, who has her master's degree in special education with endorsements in emotional impairment and learning disabilities, is someone who knows both sides of the table, as she is both an educator and a parent of an individual with autism spectrum disorder. She continues to advocate for her son as well as her students in her role as special education coordinator at Woodland Park Academy in Grand Blanc, Michigan. Mrs. Salem shares her advice:

> The relationship an educator wants with a parent or caregiver is that of a teammate. When a student has an Individual Education Plan (IEP), those of us who are involved are called an "IEP team." That team is comprised of the special education teacher, general education teacher, and other specialized team members, such as speech pathologist, social worker, occupational therapist, etc. However, the core member of that team is often overlooked—the parent(s). Most often, the parent has insights into their child that nobody else could have and is critical in developing the most effective plans to meet the student's needs. In order for this team to work most effectively on behalf of the student, there has to be communication and respect. The parent can create consistent or scheduled communication with the educators, be informed of the student's goals, and be personally involved in their child's education. A parent has the right to ask for a review of the IEP prior to the annual review. The team can meet and brainstorm possible alternatives to the current approaches.
>
> A successful partnership requires effective communication and a shared determination for the child to succeed. A parent cannot drop off their child at school and expect the teachers to be fully responsible for their child's progress toward the goal.

What is most hurtful in the relationship between a parent and a teacher is unrealistic expectations. Often a parent expects a classroom teacher or a special education teacher to have magic fairy dust that will propel their child forward and meet their every need. The whole child needs to be addressed, and that requires effort from both parents and educators. Another hindrance to a successful relationship between parents and educators is a lack of mutual respect and a lack of quality and consistent communication.

Creating well-defined expectations, and clearly expressed methods by which they are to be accomplished, is the best way to ensure all involved parties experience success. Maintaining high expectations based on mutually agreed upon goals is an essential component in supporting a student and setting them up for success; in contrast, having unrealistic goals for a student contributes to them having a negative self-image and feeling defeated.

On the other end of the spectrum, creating excuses for a student or not holding them accountable for those things they are capable of and upon which their goals are based will do a great disservice to the child. Our goal as parents and educators is to prepare the child for everyday life and give them the skills that will serve them as they grow to be successful members of the community. Lessening our expectations or not being consistent in our expectations will only confuse the child and does not give an accurate representation of what expectations and responses they will face as they enter into real-life situations.

Direct communication, preferably a conversation in a scheduled meeting or phone call, is ideal when a parent has concerns. Emails can lead to misunderstandings, and going over a teacher's head to a superior or administrator only leads to offense. Trying to squeeze in a meaningful conversation at the beginning or end of a school day with other people around is not ideal either. A teacher will be most receptive to a parent who comes to a scheduled meeting with realistic and thoughtful suggestions presented with a spirit of cooperation. A parent should share their concerns with the educators and ask if there are any situations or behaviors in the school setting that might be impacting their child's progress.

If a child with special needs already has an existing IEP, parents should keep a copy of the IEP as well as their child's progress reports and report cards from the prior year. Ask about the goals for the child and if they were met. Ask why and how the current goals were developed.

Stay as involved in your child's classroom as you can. Volunteer whenever it is feasible. Promote positive communication with the teacher. Just as parents welcome positive feedback about their child, educators also welcome positive feedback along with your concerns. Supporting the classroom teacher and sharing positive thoughts about them with your child helps create an atmosphere of respect toward the teacher.

If a parent has made an effort to communicate with the teachers or administrators and has experienced lack of cooperation, lack of response, or resistance to realistic suggestions or requests to review IEP goals and strategies on an ongoing basis, the parent has reason to be concerned. A parent is a member of their child's IEP team and has rights that a school is legally bound to uphold. A copy of parental rights is required to be issued to parents at every IEP. Copies of those rights can also be found on the internet. Be very aware of your rights and make informed decisions based on your legally mandated entitlements. You are your child's biggest advocate and their voice.

Teachers can be our greatest allies. I hope you have some great takeaways from these three amazing educators, and I hope you will come back to these pages as you seek to establish a positive relationship and partnership with your child's teacher allies.

Doctor Allies

As parents, we can view doctors either as stepping-stones to our children's health and physical development or as roadblocks and a source of frustration. Sometimes, we have a difficult time communicating with doctors and feel like we aren't being heard. We may feel insecure about asking questions, wonder if we have asked the right questions, and feel overwhelmed by the task of managing the relationships with primary care doctors, specialists, therapists, etc.

In these relationships, we have a choice: We can choose to partner with medical professionals as we watch our child develop and overcome physical limitations, or we can become frustrated, defeated, and consider giving up on the hope we once had for our child to grow in stature.

Let me start off by saying that I am a work in progress when it comes to connecting with doctor allies. As I've made mistakes and tried again, there are some things I have learned regarding Charlie's medical needs. First, I must be proactive. I need to walk into that doctor's office on the offense for my child and not the defense. I need to be ready to engage openly and honestly.

In our early years with Charlie, it seemed like every appointment drove Charlie (and me) to tears as she was restrained, poked, and prodded just to gather information and decide what the necessary care and follow-up should be. I developed a thick skin, and in many ways, a hard heart. As the appointments continued for Charlie, my heart grew harder. I walked into doctors' offices with a wall up, wanting to protect myself and my daughter. This only caused tension and added strain and stress to each visit. I needed to soften, lean in, and create an ally.

Second, I have learned that I must prepare and educate myself about my child's current needs. Preparation is so important before scheduled appointments, much like preparing for a trip to the grocery store. Maybe you are like me, and you have tried to do a quick grocery run without first checking the fridge and pantry and making a list of necessary items. You think to yourself, *Surely, I don't need a list. I will just be in and out and get what I need.* Then you get home and realize you should have gotten more coffee, you are out of eggs, and you need some toothpaste. When I walk into Charlie's appointments unprepared, I find myself coming home and regretting that I didn't take advantage of my time with the doctor to address the issues and concerns we have in the day-to-day. I must be okay with being the mom with a list. I educate myself on what routine blood work, exams, and milestones we need to pay attention to and discuss at each of Charlie's annual well-visits. I prepare my list of the things I have researched and the questions or concerns I have and carry it with me to the appointment. As mother and caretaker, I don't want to be passive or put off something that needs attention now. If I want to be Charlie's champion, I need to fight for her and support her in this way.

These final allies I share with you are amazing doctors who each have a godly, caring perspective on the health and well-being of any child.

Dr. Duane Allyn has more than thirty years of experience, and when I spoke with him, he was a member the Ascension Genesys medical team who oversaw Charlie's overall health (he has since retired). He willingly gave of his time to share about his experience with families and has some great insight for us:

> Your role as the parent of your child is that of a mother bear. Do what you feel is best for your child. You get more flies with honey, so do your best to become friends with your child's doctor and not enemies. Never feel pressured do to this or that, but always do what you feel is best for your child.
>
> I want my patients to feel like they are family. I want them to feel that they can trust me. I promise to do what is best for each child based on my experience and education. If you need to call, call. Have me in your back pocket. I am looking out for your child's best interests. Don't worry about confidentiality; parents will be informed when it is appropriate. It's a privilege to care for your child.
>
> When it comes to having questions or concerns about your child, it is best to write a list and get all your questions answered at your scheduled appointment. That way you don't walk out and wish you had asked something. Take time

to think about them and express them the way you want to, and we'll be able to go through the list quickly.

When it comes to your child's specific diagnosis and the primary care doctor's knowledge on the details of your child's care, much depends on the situation. If it is a more common genetic abnormality or diagnosis, some doctors will have a fairly good idea of the care your child needs; however, if it is a rare diagnosis, understand that the doctor will need to learn and educate themselves along with the parent. Doctors can work together within a team and pass a patient off to another doctor in the team if needed. I encourage parents to find someone who has the expertise. Try to initially make it work with your child's doctor. You must ask yourself, *Is this doctor willing to learn about my child?* If you have a doctor who is willing and trying to learn, it is worth continuing with that doctor. If it's not a good fit, get online, connect with parent groups, and find a doctor other parents use and like. But don't assume a parent suggestion is the best doctor for your child.

It is good for parents to educate themselves. I would strongly advise parents to use appropriate and valid websites. I get concerned when parents gather their medical information from invalid sources or the opinions of other parents. I love it when parents know what their child needs. If a parent does good research, they can be the ones who teach the doctors.

A parent might consider changing doctors when they don't feel like they are being heard or taken seriously. If your concerns aren't being heard, it might be time to move on. You may need a new doctor if there is a language barrier or strong accents that make it difficult to have clear and direct communication. You also may consider changing doctors if what they want seems truly inappropriate, or if you come to the point where you believe you no longer have a positive professional relationship.

> You might hurt your relationship with your child's doctor if you begin using other doctors or going to after-hours clinics (simply because it's convenient) without the knowledge of your primary care doctor. Always go to the primary care doctor first. I would encourage parents to trust that the primary care doctor knows your child best.

I love hearing from a doctor's perspective. You might realize after reading this that you are already championing in all the right ways related to your child's health, or maybe there is something you now feel encouraged to do better.

We have one more doctor ally to hear from. Dr. Renny Abraham, MD, has offered his medical expertise not only to his patients here in the States but also to patients on the mission field. His experience and wisdom can provide great insight for us as parents. Dr. Abraham specializes in internal medicine and has been pediatrics board certified since 2003. Here's what he shares from the perspective of a doctor ally:

> A successful caregiver advocate is bold. He or she does not shy away from asking difficult questions. They are also transparent about their concerns and shed light on perceived or real deficiencies in the child's well-being.
>
> Regarding the type of relationship between doctor and patient, this entirely depends on the developmental state of the child. For example, with teenagers, the relationship shifts from being parent-centered to focusing on the child taking responsibility for his or her healthcare. This independence helps the child own their healthcare. On the other end of the spectrum are children from neonates through toddlers. Their parents are the focus of all communication as they are the main advocates for their young ones.
>
> When addressing concerns or asking questions, it helps when parents come with a list of well-thought-out questions and concerns. This leads to a more fruitful dialogue. The caregiver should take advantage of any patient portal options to email non-urgent matters. They should have virtual access to their providers for more immediate concerns.

Regarding their knowledge of your child's diagnosis, your doctor should, at bare minimum, have a willingness to learn. Most primary care physicians (PCP) cannot be all things to all people. Find a PCP who has relationships with specialists who can fill in the knowledge gaps. The ideal PCP will have access to the latest medical journals and to specific specialists that help assist the PCPs. Arrogance is to be avoided at all costs, since the speed at which medical knowledge is multiplying can make most PCPs outdated in a matter of a few years.

Ideally, it's both the parent and the provider that work hand in hand to care for the child. Data is continuously being added to each disease process, so having both the parents and providers look after the best interest of the child is ideal.

Communication is key. No parent should feel shut down from sharing their concerns. A provider who makes a caregiver feel less willing to be open and honest will have a rocky relationship with them. Providing access is also important. All parents should have an easy way to communicate via email or virtually with their provider, and they should not have to wait for prolonged periods of time to see them.

A lack of transparency hurts both parties. When access and communication are impaired, then the relationship should be severed, and you should find a new doctor for your child.

Champion Challenge

I challenge you to take steps using these professionals' advice to improve your championing. Let's review some of the major takeaways:

Ally Advice from Teachers

1. Work to develop trust, respect, and good communication.
2. Partner with your child's teacher and follow through with goals and suggested activities at home.
3. Don't initiate communication when you are emotionally charged. Try to meet face-to-face with your child's teacher to discuss important issues.

4. Educate yourself before an IEP. Ask questions, come prepared with a printed copy, review goals, voice concerns, be proactive, and stay engaged in the process.
5. Remember that teachers want and need a parent's support.
6. Check your attitude. The parent's attitude and behavior toward the teacher can make a big impact on their child's success.
7. Stay involved. Your child's academic progress and success do not depend solely on the teacher; it is a shared responsibility.
8. Get involved in your child's classroom.
9. Give positive feedback when you have it.

Ally Advice from Doctors

1. Do what you feel is best for your child.
2. Bring your list of questions and concerns to your child's appointment.
3. Help educate your child's doctor as you educate yourself. Be sure to gather research from trusted sources and websites.
4. Make sure your child's doctor is willing either to learn about your child's diagnosis or connect you with another team member who has more expertise or experience regarding the needs of your child.
5. Be bold and proactive.

Our children's teachers and doctors can be our allies. As we pray for our children to grow in wisdom and stature, let's do our best to create healthy ally relationships with these professionals.

In our final chapter, we will look at the ultimate champion of all champions—the One who is our example in every way.

Chapter 10
The Ultimate Champion

We do this by keeping our eyes on Jesus, the champion who initiates and perfects our faith. Because of the joy awaiting him, he endured the cross, disregarding its shame. Now he is seated in the place of honor beside God's throne.

—Hebrews 12:2, NLT

To bring this book to a close, I want to leave you with a revelation that I believe can empower you and free you to walk in victory as a parent who wants to rise up and champion for your child. If you can believe and take hold of this revelation, you will be full of hope for your child and equipped to fulfill your calling as their advocate. Considering the title of this book, *Champion for Charlie*, I want to shine a light on the truth of who the true champion is for my daughter.

I believe with all my heart that I am called and chosen to be the mother of my children. It is my calling to love, nurture, and help Charlie, Owen, and Nora so that they might know God, love people, and find their purpose in the kingdom of God while here on this earth. The weight of who they are and what they will become goes beyond what I can carry—or what I have been asked to carry, for that matter. Though I champion every day, there is One who is the ultimate champion and who fights for each one of my children. He goes before them. He follows behind them. He is all around them every moment of every single day of their lives (Isaiah 52:12). He has no weakness. He makes no mistakes. He is the perfect champion, and His name is Jesus.

Jesus is the best champion for Charlie. As we look back on these past nine years with Charlie, we have seen her Champion (capital C) open doors for the right doctor at the right time. We have seen her Champion heal her body. We have seen her Champion protect her. We have seen her Champion fight for her. Her Champion gives us wisdom as parents when we have needed to make difficult decisions—decisions we have been scared to make because of the great impact they will have on her life.

We don't have to carry the weight of her past, present, and future circumstances; we can rest in the truth that she has the absolute greatest Champion fighting for her. Charlie's Champion is constantly working on her behalf and directing our steps as parents. Charlie's Champion is the perfect friend, counselor, provider, and defender. Jesus is the One who advocates in ways we never could, in places we will never be, among people that we may never see.

My human mind and body limit what I can do for Charlie, but Jesus has no limit to what He can do. I run out of patience and grace, but Jesus' love reaches deep and wide and has no end (Ephesians 3:18). There are places I cannot go with Charlie, but Jesus is right by her side—in her classroom, on the playground, in the lunchroom, on the bus (Psalm 16:8). He is right there with her; He never leaves and won't let her down. I will disappoint her; I will make mistakes. Jesus is perfect in all His ways (Psalm 18:30). Jesus is the ultimate Champion for Charlie.

When Charlie grows up and looks back at her life, I not only want her to see that her parents fought for her but I also want her to have an understanding that Jesus was the One who truly loved her, fought for her, and has carried her every step of the way.

Jesus is the ultimate Champion for your child as well.

Truth Be Told

The reality of who Christ is and what He does for us has the potential to lead us into a greater purpose and understanding of who we are and who our children are meant to be. When we take time to reflect on the character of Jesus and get to know and trust Him personally, He fills us with strength and hope. I want to remind you of the truth of who Jesus is and what He offers as the Champion for your spouse, your children, and for you.

Jesus Is the Son of God—Luke 22:70 (NASB): *And they all said, "Are you the Son of God, then?" And He said to them, "Yes, I am."*

Jesus was more than a good man or a prophet. He is the Son of God. And as God's Son, He walked this earth as the very image of God (Colossians 1:15). To know Jesus is to know God, and to know God is to know Jesus. Jesus, the Son of God, who formed and holds the earth and the lives of our children in His hands, is championing for our children in greater ways than we could ever understand! God loves and is advocating for our children.

He Is a Powerful Champion—Matthew 28:18 (NIV): *Then Jesus came to them and said, "All authority in heaven and on earth has been given to me."*

Jesus has all power and authority. He is able to do all things. There is nothing He can't do as He powerfully advocates for our children. What is impossible in the natural, Jesus can do because He has supernatural power and authority given to Him from His Father. The same power that created the universe is the power that is available to us through Christ Jesus. He is a powerful champion!

He Is a Miracle-Working Champion—Mark 4:41 (NASB): *They became very much afraid and said to one another, "Who then is this, that even the wind and the sea obey Him?"*

John 4:50 (ESV): *Jesus said to him, "Go; your son will live." The man believed the word that Jesus spoke to him and went on his way.*

Jesus speaks, and things happen! Jesus uses His power and authority to change situations and people so that His glory can be known. Things change when Jesus comes on the scene. He brought peace, healing, and life as He advocated for people when He walked this earth, and He still does the same today! Our Champion can do miracles.

He Is a Perfect Champion—2 Samuel 22:31 (NLT): *God's way is perfect. All the LORD's promises prove true. He is a shield for all who look to him for protection.*

There is no flaw in the way Christ champions for us. He is perfect in every single way and in every single situation. His ways for our children are perfect. His promises will not fail. And He is a perfect shield for our children and for us. Although there may be times we don't fully understand how He is working, He is doing a good and perfect work.

He Is a Selfless Champion—Ephesians 5:2 (NLT): *He loved us and offered himself as a sacrifice for us.*

Love compelled Jesus to offer Himself on the cross to pay the penalty of sin for all mankind so we might know God and live for Him and live with Him for eternity in heaven. Jesus stood in our place so we could be made right with God. He gave of Himself for our benefit. This was the greatest act of love and championing, and His championing continues as He goes before our children and fights for them.

He Is a Loving Champion—1 John 4:19 (NIV): *We love because he first loved us.*

Love motivates Jesus to champion for us. He loves our children more than we ever could. This may be hard to understand, but when we look at Jesus and the love He has for us, it is much bigger and greater than what we could ever offer, receive from another person, or even understand. This is the love that is motivating our child's perfect Champion. His love is a perfect love that comes with no conditions (Romans 5:8). His love goes deeper and stretches farther than the love we could have for our children.

He Is a Way-making Champion—Romans 3:24 (NLT): *Yet God, in his grace, freely makes us right in his sight. He did this through Christ Jesus when he freed us from the penalty for our sins.*

Jesus made things right for us. He fixed the problem of sin and death and made a way for us to be forgiven and redeemed in the sight of God. He steps in and is the answer. He can eliminate the obstacles that get in our way. He continues to fight battles for us that we never have to fight for ourselves. He is the miracle we needed for salvation, and He makes a way for the miracles we need for our children.

He Is a Creator Champion—Psalm 139:14 (NIV): *I praise you because I am fearfully and wonderfully made; your works are wonderful, I know that full well.*

Jesus sees in us what we can't always see in ourselves. He sees our potential. He sees us as wonderfully made. He is the Champion who created and designed every detail of our children—their personality, their hopes, and their dreams. He knows their fears, their perspective, and their very nature. He sees the potential in our children and knows what they are capable of. The One who made them knows fully what is possible and how to come alongside and advocate for them.

He Is the Overcoming Champion—John 16:33 (NIV): *I have told you these things, so that in me you may have peace. In this world you will have trouble. But take heart! I have overcome the world.*

We may have days we want to quit. But the perfect Champion will never quit! We get tired, but He never does! He never stops championing! It is His nature to overcome! He never stops working, never stops moving, and never stops defending and protecting our children.

Knowing the truth about Jesus brings life and hope to our hearts as parents advocating for our children. He is the perfect Champion. Yes, we will choose to rise up. We will pray hard. We will have the grit of gratitude and go from strength to strength. We will link arms with parents and fellow allies to help us champion. But the greatest advantage we have as parents is the Champion who came to this earth, who gave His life for me and for you, and who reigns in heaven, where He is still fighting for us!

Parent with Peace

The truth of who Jesus is can change the way we parent and champion. Though I strive to protect, support, and advocate for Charlie, I find great peace in the fact that Charlie's life rests in the hands of the One who gifted her to our family. She belongs to Jesus.

I can trust Jesus with Charlie's every need. He is the One who knows her inside and out. He knit her together in my womb and created her for a purpose that He sees in full view. My understanding is limited, but nothing is hidden from Him (Psalm 139:15).

With Charlie's difficulty to communicate, there are things she won't or can't tell us. Many days she comes home from school, and as we ask her about her day, she is only able to give us bits and pieces, so much remains a mystery. If it wasn't for a great parent-teacher relationship, I would know very little about Charlie's activity in the classroom and among her peers. When it comes to her thoughts, her feelings, and her worries, I am often left wondering. But Jesus—the One who knows her inside and out, knows her every thought, and watches over her every day—is with her. Her Champion knows her even better than she knows herself. Relying upon the One who made her and can champion for her in every way brings me so much peace.

When I realize that I am not championing alone but that the perfect Champion is also at work—always at work—I can parent with peace. Our children have a perfect Champion. I hope this truth does for you what it does for me. It takes the weight off my heart and shoulders. It allows me to breathe and rest in His power and strength. Parenting under the constant pressure to make the perfect decisions at the perfect time can create unnecessary and unhealthy tension and stress. Let's choose to trust Jesus and not carry the weight of advocating alone.

I Can't, but He Can

No one is the perfect parent. None of us of can say we have done it all right all the time. There is much we need to learn. Sometimes I pray that my young kids don't remember the mistakes I've made in their early years!

I will never forget the time I had Charlie with me out grocery shopping. I had finished checking out, gathered my grocery bags, and walked out to my car. I left my cart neatly pushed in with the other carts on the way out the door. I loaded my groceries in the car, and as I pulled open the driver's side door, I had the feeling I was forgetting something. My heart dropped when I realized the *something* I had forgotten was my daughter. I had left Charlie in the cart inside the store. I quickly ran back inside to find her safe and sound, resting in her carrier in the cart. It was a total mom fail. My stomach still turns as I relive that experience. I felt like the worst mother ever. I'm pretty sure I am one of the reasons stores offer curbside pickup. It's a great way to keep from leaving a child behind at the store.

This is just one of several stories I could share of how I have fallen short as a parent. The truth is, I can't be the perfect mom. I will do the wrong thing. I mess up. But thankfully, championing for our children is not all about what we can do as parents. We can't do it all, but their perfect Champion can. He can do far above what we can do. Our children's greatest needs are not met in our parenting but in their Champion and Savior, Jesus.

I can't be everything for Charlie, but He can. He can be there for her when I can't. He can open doors I can't. He can bring favor and soften hearts that I can't. Where I have limits, He is limitless (Job 36:22).

Hit the Bullseye

Our fellow advocates can inspire us. I admire so many parents who continue to rise up and advocate for their children. They have great wisdom, they are so passionate, and they are the trailblazers for the rest of us. It is great to learn from other people, like those who have shared their insights with us in this book. Their stories spur us on, and our stories can do the same for them. Advocate and ally connections can help us grow in our ability to effectively champion for our kids. But if I want to hit the bullseye as a parent, I don't look to people alone.

Rather than looking to other moms' or influencers' examples as the target for what I should be doing, my primary target is Christ. I need to look to Christ as the example in how I ought to advocate for my children. He is the constant mark and target that is always perfect. When Christ is the example for my advocacy, I will hit the bullseye every time.

Christ has set the example for us in how to live. His life here on earth was all about advocating and championing for people. He not only walked this earth as a champion but continues to champion for us before our Father in heaven, making intercession for us. Romans 8:34 says that Jesus is "at the right hand of God interceding [with the Father] for us." He is constantly championing for us to God in heaven, making requests and petitions on our behalf. Isn't that incredible?

When Jesus is our example in our championing, we will always get it right. He is the ultimate and perfect Champion. I encourage you to open your Bible and read about the life of Jesus. See how He loved, how He spoke, how He served, how He led with passion and purpose. As you get to know Jesus and how He lived while on the earth, you will be inspired in how to live your life and fulfill your calling to champion for our child. Aim for Jesus, and you will hit the bullseye!

Make Him Your Champion

I hope that as I have shared about my journey and our family's experience, we have made a meaningful connection that inspires you not only to rise up and advocate but also to know Jesus in a greater and deeper way. I pray that you choose to make Him your champion. He is ready and willing not just to be the champion for your child but to be your champion as well. He wants you to know Him and the truth of who He is. You can embrace Him as the Son of God and welcome Him into your life so that He can show His power and work miracles in and through you. As you accept Him and put your trust in Him, you will be filled with His love and see Him make a way for you to live with purpose and for His glory.

My friend, if you want to live your life in the arms of our ultimate Champion, it is as simple as pausing in this moment and opening up your heart to Jesus. You can choose to put down this book and say a simple prayer. I urge you not to wait for the perfect moment or to think that you must first get your life in order. It doesn't matter where you are or that you say the perfect words. As you give your life to Him, Jesus is ready to be your champion.

If you have surrendered your life to Jesus before, but it's been awhile since you have felt close to Jesus, you can pray and welcome Him back as Champion once again. Our Champion always welcomes us back. His mercy and grace draw us to Himself over and over again. If you want to make Him your Champion and accept Him as your Savior, you can say a simple prayer like this . . .

Jesus, today I give my life to You. I believe that You are the Son of God, and I want You to be my Savior and Champion. I need You; I can't do life without You. I'm sorry for doing things in my own strength, in my own way. Today I give You my heart and my family. Come into my life and lead me in Your ways. I want to know You more. In Jesus' name, amen.

It's as simple as believing in your heart and confessing with your mouth. My friend, you can live this life with peace knowing that your ultimate Champion and Savior, Jesus Christ, is always with you.

It's Time to Shine

My prayer is that this book has encouraged you and allowed God to work in your heart. I hope you didn't just underline a few phrases and dog-ear a few pages, but that you were impacted by what God wanted to say to you and do in your family. I have prayed for you. I have prayed that you who need healing would have the grace and strength to rise up with renewed purpose and passion. I have prayed that you who have been hurting or grown weary would be reenergized to get back in the race and move forward with fresh perspective and an excitement for what is possible in the future.

God desires for each of us to be filled with hope so that we might rise up and live as those chosen to champion for our children. I pray that through what you've read, you feel better equipped to advocate; but ultimately I pray that you choose to trust, believe in, and rest in the Champion of all champions. Jesus has your child and your family in His hands, and He sees you. Trust in His goodness and His power to work all things according to His good plans and purpose.

> *And we know that in all things God works for the good of those who love him, who have been called according to his purpose.*
> —*Romans 8:28, NIV*

As we champion *with Christ* and *in Christ*, may He shine through our lives and the lives of our children! This life is not about me, and it's not about my child; it's about Christ revealed in me so that others might see and know Him.

My friend, it's time to shine. To God be the glory!

Advocate Resources

Jen Forsthoff
jenforsthoff.com
Stay connected with Jen and Charlie and be encouraged in your journey of faith and championing. Contact Jen for details if you wish to schedule a speaking engagement.

Joni and Friends
joniandfriends.org
Changing the church and communities around the world. Find *Family Retreat* opportunities to enjoy time away with your family while being spiritually and physically refreshed.

Nathaniel's Hope
nathanielshope.org
Find *Buddy Break* opportunities through Nathaniel's Hope. This respite program offers parents a break while celebrating kids with special needs.

Tim Tebow Foundation
timtebowfoundation.org
Exists to bring faith, hope, and love to those needing a brighter day in their darkest hour of need. The Night to Shine event is one of the Tim Tebow Foundation programs.

St. Jude Children's Research Hospital
stjude.org
St. Jude has programs to help families with children who have complex medical problems.

National Down Syndrome Society
ndss.org
The leading human rights organization for all individuals with Down syndrome. Find healthcare guidelines for your child's annual well-visits and for being proactive with their development.

AMBUCS
ambucs.org
In more than thirty states across America, AMBUCS works to inspire mobility and independence through their Amtryke Therapeutic Tricycle Program. (Charlie received an Amtryke when she was three as a tool for physical therapy and for learning to ride a bike.)

Bedwetting Store
bedwettingstore.com
Great tool for finding support and resources to help your child.

Local Resources

Below are a few Michigan-based organizations I love. Local and state programs can offer great connections and be a valuable source of information. Search online for additional resources in your state, county, or community.

Cornerstone Church
cornerstonehighland.com
If you are looking for a local church in southeast Michigan, join our family at Cornerstone Church in Highland.

Early On
1800earlyon.org
Early intervention services in Michigan for infants and toddlers from birth to three years of age with developmental delays or disabilities and their families. (Both of my daughters have received free therapies and support through this program.)

Michigan Alliance for Families
michiganallianceforfamilies.org
MAF provides support, information, and education for families who have children and young adults who receive special education services.

Michigan Parents of Children with Down Syndrome
Social media group on Facebook.com
Find a place to ask your questions and get feedback and support from local parents who are raising a child with Down syndrome.

Clarkston Scamp
clarkstonscamp.org
A special place for special kids! This is a local summer camp that Charlie has loved participating in the past several years. This camp is designed for campers ages three to forty.

Acknowledgments

To my Ultimate Champion, my King and Savior, Jesus Christ: In Your perfect plan, You gifted us with Charlie and chose us to be her champions. You are the One who truly authored this book because You are authoring our lives and journey as a family. You are my firm foundation, Your promises fuel my purpose, and as You call me to greater levels of surrender, I want to live for Your glory.

To my husband, best friend and co-champion of our children: Thank you for your support and love from the moment I first shared my burden to write this book. For the hours I snuck away to write, rewrite, and labor over these pages, thank you for praying, encouraging, and seeing me through every moment I needed you in my corner. There is no one else I would rather be on this parenting journey with than you. You lead and love our family so well.

To those who supported the publishing of this book, our precious family, friends: Your financial support, prayers, and encouragement have carried this message from a burden in my heart to a book in the hands of those who need hope to rise up and advocate for their child.

To those who contributed to the content of *Champion for Charlie*—Natalie Gecele, Chris Salem, Christine Conroy, Jen Jones, Pam Chandler, Becky Monte, Heather Mannor, Dr. Renny Abraham, Dr. Duane Allyn: You are helping parents better advocate for their children. The wisdom you have shared will allow parents to push their child further so they can succeed academically, physically, spiritually, emotionally, and socially.

To Erin Casey and her team: It has been an honor and a joy to participate in this project with you. Thank you for the time, energy, and care you have invested into every page of *Champion for Charlie*. Thank you for believing in this message and making it beautiful and accessible for readers.

To my fellow champions, who are fighting, believing, and praying for their child: You are called, you are chosen to advocate for your child's purpose and destiny here on earth, and by God's grace, you will be equipped. Don't give up—rise up and be the champion your child needs you to be.

About the Author

Jen Forsthoff brings hope and life to readers by using her experiences raising a daughter with Down syndrome to advocate for parents of special-needs children and communicate biblical truths that will encourage them in their journey. She strives to bring spiritual breakthrough and victory for every parent and individual entrusted with a special-needs child and desires to invite others to live each day fulfilling their purpose and calling as parents chosen to champion for their child.

Jen lives in Fenton, Michigan, with her husband, Lucas, and their three children: Charlotte (9), Owen (6), and Nora (4). She passionately fulfills her calling to ministry at Cornerstone Church, where she serves alongside Lucas as a worship leader, young adults ministry leader, and support staff. She earned her degree in elementary education from Oral Roberts University and uses her education and experience—in the classroom, among families, and in ministry—to effectively communicate a life-giving message to readers. As a community and state advocate for children with special needs, she seeks opportunities to make a difference and have a positive impact by helping meet the practical and spiritual needs of those around her. Jen longs to see others rise up as champions chosen for their child while placing their hope in Christ and the truth of His Word.